From Barrenness to Fruitfulness

ↄ

The scope of this book far exceeds any roadblock,
devastation or frustration posed by times of barrenness
in our lives. Frank Damazio writes with wisdom and
sensitivity to help open the doors of blessing for pastors,
churches, couples and individuals who have yet to see
the full release of fruitfulness in their lives. I highly
recommend *From Barrenness to Fruitfulness*.

Ché Ahn

Senior Pastor, Harvest Rock Church
President, Harvest International Ministries
Pasadena, California

"All day I faced the barren waste without a taste of water...."
Frank Damazio's book *From Barrenness to Fruitfulness*
encourages churches and individuals to "face the barren
waste" with hope and faith. Such a stance could bring
revival and vitality back to the Church at just the right time.
Damazio has birthed another significant contribution to
the cause of Christ and the coming of His kingdom. I
recommend you read it with an open, seeking heart and
let God use it as a surgical tool to remove barrenness,
restore vitality and recover your vision.

Joe C. Aldrich

President, Multnomah Bible College
Portland, Oregon

Praise for
From Barrenness to Fruitfulness

With grace and compassion, Frank Damazio walks us
through a masterful study of Scripture—and his own
personal experience—to provide us comfort and hope
in seasons of barrenness. A great book!

Ed Silvoso
President, Harvest Evangelism
San Jose, California

As a pastor, to be evangelistic, growing and alive are my
only options. *From Barrenness to Fruitfulness* is a clear
and powerful treatment of the subject.

Casey Treat
Pastor, Christian Faith Center
Seattle, Washington

Fresh, creative, vivid and deeply insightful,
From Barrenness to Fruitfulness is the word of the
day for American churches.

C. Peter Wagner
Fuller Theological Seminary
Colorado Springs, Colorado

From Barrenness to Fruitfulness

Frank Damazio

Regal

A Division of Gospel Light
Ventura, California, U.S.A.

Published by Regal Books
A Division of Gospel Light
Ventura, California, U.S.A.
Printed in U.S.A.

Regal Books is a ministry of Gospel Light, an evangelical Christian publisher dedicated to serving the local church. We believe God's vision for Gospel Light is to provide church leaders with biblical, user-friendly materials that will help them evangelize, disciple and minister to children, youth and families.

It is our prayer that this Regal book will help you discover biblical truth for your own life and help you meet the needs of others. May God richly bless you.

For a free catalog of resources from Regal Books and Gospel Light please call your Christian supplier, or contact us at 1-800-4-GOSPEL or at www.gospellight.com.

Cover Design by Kevin Keller
Interior Design by Britt Rocchio
Edited by Karen Kaufman

Library of Congress Cataloging-in-Publication Data
Damazio, Frank
    From barrenness to fruitfulness / Frank Damazio.
        p. cm.
    Includes bibliographical references.
    ISBN 0-8307-2337-4 (hardcover).
    1. Christian leadership. 2. Infertility—Biblical teaching.
    3. Infertility—Religious aspects—Christianity. I Title.
    BV652.1.D35 1998   98-19263
    253—dc21   CIP

1 2 3 4 5 6 7 8 9 10 11 12 13 14 15 16 17 18 19 20 / 04 03 02 01 00 99 98

Rights for publishing this book in other languages are contracted by Gospel Literature International (GLINT). GLINT also provides technical help for the adaptation, translation and publishing of Bible study resources and books in scores of languages worldwide. For further information, write to GLINT at P.O. Box 4060, Ontario, CA 91761-1003, U.S.A. You may also send e-mail to Glintint@aol.com, or visit their web site at www.glint.org.

I dedicate this book to my family,
especially to my wife, Sharon, who experienced
the sorrow of barrenness and the joy of fruitfulness.
Without her, this book would not have been
written. And to our four special gifts:
Nicole and Bethany, miracle gifts of love and life,
and Andrew and Jessica, mercy gifts
of surprise and enjoyment.

Contents

◔

CHAPTER 1

A Personal Journey Through the School of Barrenness

Disappointment and grief are not the end;
they only provide opportunities for life to be
produced in unexpected ways.

CHAPTER 2

A Biblical Understanding of Barrenness

Barrenness is God's secret school of success, producing a
healthy offering of humility, faith, patience and hope.

CHAPTER 3

Congregational Spiritual Abortions and Miscarriages

Churches need recovery times after spiritual abortions
and miscarriages. Leaders who attempt to force birth only
cause more wounding.

Foreword

○

For decades now, I have been privileged to pastor a congregation of a size church which analysts describe as a "megachurch." The irony of this fact is that not only did we not set out to "build a big church," but we have refused to suggest anything of a superior role associated with such large churches or to suppose that a superior wisdom on our part has contributed to the phenomenon of our size.

Whatever God's purpose for large, multi-thousand congregations, there is one thing I feel certain it is *not*. Unfortunately, to my view, that *"not"* thing seems to be what happens most as observers look at megachurches. They become <u>icons</u>: images of success that many earnest leaders hope to emulate, or worse—idols of methodology motivated by a leader's almost desperate quest for fruitfulness, and too often, in the frenetic pursuit of goals sincerely sought, the pursuit goes unfulfilled. More, the deepest motives of the leader go undiscerned.

Of course, motives are rarely intentionally unworthy—especially among spiritual leaders. Still, while our minds insist that the service of God and the salvation of souls are our one consuming passion, unperceived to ourselves is the fact that our hearts are often dominated by fears of failure—by a crying inner need to find an effective, multiplying church ministry for undiscerned reasons. Thus, though hardly noticing it of ourselves, we who lead too often crave fruitfulness that thereby we might gain something other than true "spiritual fruit." So often our insecurities, intensified by constant feelings of being compared with our peers, are actually seeking a verification of our worth; our anxious labors seeking to gain some evidence of divine approval or affirmation through our being distinguished in the eyes of those who view our ministries.

It is painfully common. I know, for the first several years of my own ministry garnered little visible fruit and, accordingly, were clouded with a recurring guilt borne of the notion that "something's wrong with me." Such a state exposes the soul to so many temptations; to the potential for jealousy toward fruitful ministries we see around us; to a vulnerability for attempting to employ exploitive or manipulative techniques in order to inveigle some semblance of "growth"—whatever the cost. Worse yet, there is a horrendous possibility of our barrenness bringing a deep-seated bitterness to lurk at the edges of our souls.

In the face of such real threats to good and godly men and women—people so devotedly submitted to answer God's call on their lives and so faithfully serving their segment of the Great Shepherd's flock—this excellent book appears.

There are not words strong enough to express the depth of my delight with Frank Damazio's work here, or the height of my hopes for a widespread distribution of its important message. *This book is at once a healing therapy and a ministry-releasing instrument.*

Having examined it, I have determined to make it a key resource in my regular Consultations at the Jack W. Hayford School of Pastoral Nurture, now located at The King's Seminary here in Van Nuys.

I want to urge church leaders to secure copies to share with hurting brothers and sisters who are discouraged over their relative lack of fruitfulness—especially those suffering from the *icon* syndrome I previously mentioned—or near to giving up hope of ever finding the joy of a harvest season in their ministries.

But there is yet another reason for reading this book.

Even the very fruitful leader, who experiences the richest of blessings in his or her ministry, would do well to study this volume's excellent content. There is rich material herein—biblical insights that have already precipitated yet-to-be-preached sermons in my own mind. The prophetic edge of the truth Frank has shared here, joined to the solid, scholarly approach he has employed in researching the idea of barrenness, affords abundant help for you or me in seeking to comfort, to console or to bring hope to souls who are suffering *any* order of barrenness in their lives or circumstances.

Before seeing this book, I was already cognizant of the fact that God's hand is on Frank Damazio; already making him one of the rising voices to speak to a new generation of pastors and other spiritual leaders. But what I was not aware of was the unique degree of divine grace God has poured forth into this vessel—or the cost he and his family have paid to be open to the possibilities that grace has brought about through them.

I believe you will be greatly blessed to share my discoveries in the many ways I have reflected on—ways that this book may bring fresh fruitfulness to our souls...and thereby, your ministry.

Jack W. Hayford
The Church On The Way
The King's Seminary

Van Nuys, California
May 1998

Acknowledgments

●

Many thanks to Kyle Duncan, who consistently encouraged my new relationship with Regal Books as a writer, and was refreshing in his transparency as a professional.

Many thanks to Bill Greig III for his vision to produce spiritually cutting-edge materials that encourage local churches worldwide toward spiritual health.

I want to especially thank Karen Kaufman, an unusually sweet and gifted editor. She was a joy to work with throughout the whole project. Thank you, Karen!

And to my secretaries, Heather Schefter and Cheryl Bolton, for going beyond the call of duty in their detailed help and determination.

Introduction

As a pastor I have deep feelings for women who cannot have children. Having walked through the pain and frustration of barrenness in my own marriage, I am now very selective with my words, my tone of voice, my facial expressions, any way I might be misread. I try to pray with sensitivity and compassion, and I pray with some level of personal understanding and faith.

I have the same feelings when I speak to pastors of a barren ministry or a barren church. Nothing works for them. They embrace new church growth ideas, methods and attitudes. They try a new seeker-sensitive approach, a new media ministry, a new worship style, but the church is not changing, growing or showing signs of spiritual life. This book is for these barren ministries, first to give an understanding of the biblical view of barrenness that will assist them in their faith journey; second, to encourage them by explaining the causes, remedies and seasons of barrenness as a natural element in leading God's people.

When the bands of barrenness broke in the Damazio household, we were still thinking and living as if we were barren. God had turned our captivity, but we had not fully accepted it. This is a significant spiritual truth that I have seen with many churches that are unable to produce. God moves to break the bands, but the leaders still live with a barren mind-set.

First the natural, then the spiritual, is a commonly understood spiritual principle among Bible-believing people. Scripture uses natural birth to explain spiritual birth, physical travail to explain spiritual travail, natural blindness to represent spiritual blindness, emotional hard-heartedness to represent spiritual hardness. The Bible is filled with first the natural and then the spiritual. There are lessons to be learned from natural barrenness and numerous applications to the whole subject of spiritual barrenness.

Join me as I share the lessons learned at the Master's feet, with the Bible as my textbook, my family as my classroom and the knowledge that He is working on behalf of His loved ones to see that all will graduate from the School of Barrenness.

1

A Personal Journey Through the School of Barrenness

○

Hope deferred makes the heart sick, but when
the desire comes, it is a tree of life.

—*Proverbs* 13:12

When my colleague asked, "When are you and Sharon going to start your family?" the question seemed awkward. Having children was, in my mind, a matter of personal choice. Like most young couples, we wanted to see marital maturity, financial stability, and have our lives in order before becoming parents.

I was 27—the right age—with good health and plenty of time to think about producing a family. My life was busy, teaching full-time at Portland Bible College and functioning as an elder at our home church. College life was full and demanding, especially when I taught 16 credit hours the first year. I poured over my books from early morning until late at night. Sharon was 24, and fulfilled as a full-time legal secretary, working for a progressive law firm in downtown Portland. The firm was encouraging Sharon to add more training through college and special seminars to become a paralegal.

We were in no hurry for children, but we were aware that our body clocks were ticking. Sharon's desire leaned toward family, children and creating a warm, nurturing home. She was a marvelous homemaker and an excellent seamstress, making many of her own clothes. She loved housekeeping, cooking, decorating and doing crafts. Sharon was custom-made for motherhood and we both agreed it was time to have children. Little did we know, however, that this decision would begin one of the most emotionally painful journeys of our adult lives.

Barrenness, the Breeding Ground for Guilt and Blame

After two years of no pregnancy for no apparent reason, we began to consider the possibility that the problem was infertility, impotence or other related issues.

We struggled through a range of self-guilt feelings: *If only we hadn't been so busy. Stress has changed our bodies. We've done something wrong and God is trying to get our attention. We can't be trusted with children, so God in His wisdom is withholding them from us.*

We also began to entertain thoughts of spiritual harassment through evil powers: *The devil, his demons and evil forces must be harassing our home and resisting God's blessing for us. Where did we allow satanic infiltration? What sin is lurking at our door that would draw in demonic attack? What can we do to receive deliverance or protection from this attack?*

The questions went unanswered. The only thing we had too much of was advice. Some concerned friends tried to encourage us: "Nothing is wrong. It's just God's timing. Don't be anxious." Others were more solution oriented: "Let's examine your attitudes toward children, marriage, God and life." Then came the counsel that God had predestined us to be without children in order to do His will without any distractions. The emotional hurt coupled with our unanswered spiritual questions caused us no small amount of personal turmoil.

Our initial pain was only the beginning of a 12-year journey that would change our lives, deepen our compassion for others and reveal an amazing perspective on the parallel between natural barrenness and spiritual barrenness. Barren leaders, barren churches, barren denominations, barren ministries—all would become issues I would minister to with a great deal of love, understanding and genuine answers.

We started reading books, magazine articles, pamphlets and medical research papers concerning barrenness and discovered that infertility affects one out of every six couples. Our bookshelves were lined with titles such as *Infertility: Causes and Treatments*, *Infertility at the Time of Diagnosis* and *If You're Suffering from Impotence, You're Not Alone.*

Our next step was to begin a series of regular medical examinations to pinpoint a possible problem. This was no easy task! Both my wife and I submitted to a variety of tests that were embarrassing some of the time and annoying most of the time. We closely followed all medical advice and went through what at that time seemed to be the answer. Another year passed...still no reason for the infertility...still no pregnancy, just a very distraught couple.

Groping for Grace

Our names were held up in prayer throughout the world, and my traveling ministry opened up opportunities for an outpouring of unsolicited counsel, prophecy and spiritual insight. We had numerous words predicting children. Some words were a "dealings of God" type: God is not finished breaking you, humbling you, showing you where your source really lies, removing pride from your lives and birthing a message through your ministry that could come no other way.

For several years I awakened to a weeping wife. Sharon had

her own questions: "Where is God? Why, God? Why me? If Frank is such a man of God, why doesn't the Lord hear his prayers?"

I then would move into first the "humble husband" role: "Don't worry, Honey, it'll work out. Many people have gone through this. There's nothing wrong with you or me. God loves us and has a great plan for our lives!" But I didn't know the plan and I didn't sound too convincing, so I would then transition to the "confident teacher" role: "The Bible says God wants us to multiply, to bless us with offspring. A happy home involves children." I gave her my basic Bible teaching that God hears and answers prayer, that God's timing is usually not our timing and that God will reveal to us in due season the purpose behind this testing. All trials have a short life span and it will come to pass soon, etc., etc....

On and on I would confidently speak. But the message was getting old after three, four, five years. I was getting tired of saying it, and my wife was getting tired of hearing it. Something needed to change. I was quickly becoming a "frustrated husband" and a "doubtful teacher." We couldn't ignore the problem. Children were everywhere, and by now all of our friends had one or two offspring. It was painful.

The pain was exacerbated with every joyful announcement of a friend's pregnancy, every invitation to a newborn baby shower, every instance when a friend pushed a new baby into our arms and unknowingly began to joke about our lack of children: "When are you going to start a family? Don't you like children?" Those were very hard moments, such a normal part of life and yet so discouraging and deeply hurtful for us.

Sharon and I were frustrated, tired, irritated and finally beginning to think, *Maybe children, family and a normal life isn't for us. God obviously has a different future for us.* After a few more emotional roller coaster rides with doctors, friends, prophets and counselors, we decided we had gone as far as we could. No more doctors, counseling or further pursuit. We would rest and enjoy God, continue to develop a strong marital relationship and learn to live with our *unchanging circumstances.*

Bearing the Burden for the Barren

During this period I was asked to minister at a certain church for special meetings. *Easy enough*, I thought. *I'm available to teach; they need my teaching; I'll go.* So I went. But I was unprepared for the way the Holy Spirit would so clearly speak to me during the worship service. A loud inner voice said, "Pray for all the barren women here in this service."

My response was quick and final, "NO! No, I am not going to pray for or say anything about barren women."

The Holy Spirit continued, a strong impression, a deep feeling, an inaudible voice, "Pray for the barren women."

Finally the pastor announced me as the speaker. I was on. What about this strong impression to pray for the one thing I had no faith for? I was actually a little miffed at God for bringing up the subject. Why would God ask me to do something for which I had no tangible results and no apparent faith?

The Holy Spirit won. I simply took about three minutes, and made a few comments that were anything but faith building: "If God decides to....If you have faith....I don't expect anything to happen....But I will pray and obey God."

I then prayed for at least 14 barren women. The experience was soon forgotten until I returned to the same church about 18 months later. You're probably ahead of me on this. You're right. God moved miraculously and several newborn babies were presented to me by ecstatic new moms. I was a hero, so to speak. What a faith-filled meeting we had! But I left that service more bewildered than ever. *How did that happen? Why did that happen?*

God was beginning to use my natural circumstance to work spiritually for other people. I began a long journey of biblical study about barrenness. I wondered, *Does this subject have a natural and spiritual side to it?* The more I studied, the more convinced I became that God was using our barrenness for His purposes, just as He had for the many barren men and women mentioned in Scripture.

A New Focus

Sharon and I took our attention off of our barrenness and made plans to build a family through adoption. It felt right. It was a biblical concept and we were now on a new road. But like most uncharted courses, the path is often paved with the unexpected. The adoption journey was no exception. Once again we found ourselves on a strange tour into another world of God's dealings. We thought it would be so easy, so blessed of God. It was not.

As we began our inquiries, I noticed my attitude changing toward people who were aborting their children. I began to take it personally. Every time I heard the word "abortion," I would become irritated to a low-burning anger. Here we were suffering! We would have done anything to have a child and people were killing them every day all around us. It was heartbreaking. We wanted the children to live; instead death was their destiny. It was so unfair, so cruel.

I was haunted by unanswered questions: *Why doesn't God step in and do something to stop all these abortions? Why doesn't God give children to godly people who will love them and raise them in His house?* The paradox was sometimes overwhelming.

I had to continually return to the truth of His Word. God is sovereign. God is just. God is love. God is long-suffering. God works all things after the counsel of His will. We only see the natural, the obvious. We miss the invisible and hidden truth. God really is in charge of everything and everyone, but His ways are higher than our ways, His thoughts different than our thoughts. I concluded that while we might not be able to stop abortion, we could adopt the unwanted. So we did.

Disappointment Becomes His Appointment

Our first adoption was long, costly, frustrating and a lesson in life. We adopted a little girl from Guatemala through some God-type connections and circumstances. Sharon and I were now pastoring our own church in Eugene, Oregon, which we had pioneered one year before. The whole congregation entered into the excitement of the adoption process with us, and everyone was encouraging and helpful. It was a wonderful season.

The nursery was furnished and decorated, and the closet was full of baby clothes. Our church membership numbered about 200 and was growing rapidly. We were covered with prayer and steeped in love. The time to finalize the paperwork finally came and we were ready to open our hearts and home to a six-week-old baby.

Our disappointment and grief was not the end; it was only an opportunity for tree stumps to receive new life.

We had planned on going down to Guatemala after our return from a conference in Australia where I was to speak. Sharon had already left for Australia to join her parents there, and I would wait until Monday morning to leave, so I could preach at our church on Sunday. Saturday night about 9:00 P.M. the call came from Guatemala. I can still remember the hesitation in the voice of the caller as she explained, "I don't know how to say this, but I must. Your baby daughter died a few hours ago in her crib. We don't know why. We're very sorry."

I don't recall much more of the conversation than that. My mind was racing. *How? Why? Not now! What about the church? Sharon? Our hard work? Our money? Time? Emotion? What will we do now?* I put the phone down, stood up and began pacing back and forth in my office. At first I was numb, silent. Then tears and frustration came. Finally I turned to prayer and praise. It began to flow out of me like a river. God was there and I was being ministered to. I knew everything would work out. I didn't know how, but I knew God was working.

A Scripture from the book of Job came to my mind: "For there is hope for a tree, if it is cut down, that it will sprout again, and that its tender shoots will not cease. Though its root may grow old in the earth, and its stump may die in the ground, yet at the scent of *water* it will bud and bring forth branches like a plant" (Job 14:7-9, italics added). This verse was my seed of hope. I was like that tree cut down.

Our vision and hope for children had been cut off, but all we needed was a drop of God's *water*, a drop of His mercy and love, a drop of His presence and our tree would sprout again. Our disappointment and grief was not the end; it was only an opportunity for tree stumps to receive new life. My wife received the drop of God's water when I told her the news in person at the Melbourne airport in Australia.

That night in the first meeting of the pastors' conference, Sharon sang a song spontaneously for that moment and at that moment. It was a song that inspired the pastors to receive new hope for their tree stumps. She sang Isaiah 54:1-3. Through her tears, the heart of God was imparted. We prayed for pastors needing a drop of water on their dead stumps, dead ministries, dead visions. God moved deeply. Again I was aware that God was using our barrenness to minister to barren leaders and barren churches.

New Branches from Dead Stumps

The Lord was at work in our adoption. Within several months we had another little Guatemalan girl in our arms. Our journey to pick her up in Guatemala was another series of supernatural events. God made a way where there was no way. Our first child, Nicole Ruth Damazio, was finally living in our house. She would be a Ruth because she would leave her people and be joined to us by the sovereign hand of God. At the time of this writing Nicole is 15 years old, healthy, happy, saved, water baptized, filled with the Spirit and greatly involved in our youth-evangelism activities. What a little miracle!

Another branch began to emerge. God was at work to put one more little life in our hands. We had been talking about another child, but we had no idea it would happen so quickly. Two years later a second little girl, only three days old, came to us. Her birth parents were street kids: both 15, both on drugs, both in need of Christ. We gratefully took the little girl after some legal complications and adopted her into our family. Her name is Bethany Michelle Damazio. Bethany is now 13 years old and is thriving in school, intellectually bright and musically talented. She loves God and is called to do more than she would ever imagine. We were now a family of four, thankful to God for trusting us with two "arrows" to train and guide.

At that point Sharon and I were content. We had no idea that our family tree would ever bring forth another tender shoot. It was the spring of 1987, and I was the morning speaker for a pastors' conference in Portland, Oregon. The series of messages I gave at the conference followed the theme of "Breaking the Bands of Barrenness."

The conference went extremely well with some wonderful times of prayer and personal ministry to barren pastors and barren churches. Little did I know that as I spoke on this subject, my wife discovered she was pregnant. Yes, pregnant! We had no further expectations about natural-born children, but God was breaking our natural bands of barrenness as I was breaking spiritual bands of barrenness. Sharon and I were shocked, but accepted the pregnancy as a bona fide miracle of God.

Pregnancy and childbirth became a very intense experience. From the time of the first ultrasound, showing our baby moving...through the amazing expansion of Sharon's stomach...to that moment of birth when the doctor handed me our beautiful baby boy with lots of black hair and said, "You have a son," we were both ecstatically happy and overwhelmed at God's goodness and gift to us.

Andrew David Damazio was born January 12, 1988, just a few months before our twelfth wedding anniversary. Now 10 years old, Andrew is active and full of life with an outgoing personality. He loves God, people, animals and sports! Once more, it seemed the family was complete.

Four years passed. We were busy with three children, our home, friends and a growing church. Life was good. Then to our amazement, Sharon discovered that she was pregnant again. There was no mistaking the signs. We had just celebrated 15 years of marriage. The kids were getting older, the girls were enjoying school and Andrew was leaving the toddler stage. We were looking forward to some quiet family time. Suddenly, panic! Another baby? Sharon and I looked at each other in wonder: How can we take care of four children? The timing is all wrong. We're not in our 20s anymore! And four children is a BIG family. Can we do it?

We had no idea what a joy our little girl, Jessica Faith Damazio, would be—not only to us, but also to everyone around her. Jessica was born on April 22, 1992, and is looking forward to first grade this fall. It's amazing to see yourself in your children, and Andrew and Jessica definitely have our genes.

After Jessica's birth we began to pray again, but this time our prayer was, "Lord, four is enough! We would like to retract some of the thousands of prayers for Damazio children that are still lying before Your throne."

Lessons from the School of Barrenness

When the bands of barrenness finally broke, we realized that the Master had birthed more than biological children through us; He had given us powerful teaching tools to help others graduate from the School of Barrenness. Let's recap some of the lessons we have discovered in this chapter:

- God is aware of your problem.
- Distant relatives of Job's friends will visit, but only God can bring forth life.
- God works most powerfully through our greatest points of weakness. Don't let barrenness stop you from giving.
- God will make a way, but it's not always the easy way.

- If at first you don't receive, keep trusting.
- Hope in the Lord, not in your circumstances. Dead stumps can bud again.
- Contentment allows God room to work.

((Making It Personal))

1. God cannot fill a womb that is already full or a mind that is already made up. What are some of the pre "conceived" plans you have had for your ministry?
2. Are you willing to "adopt" new plans or ideas that did not originate in you?
3. God's power is seen greatest in weakness. To whom will you minister in the area of your greatest need?
4. In what ways have you refused to be content with where you are?

2

A Biblical Understanding of Barrenness

○

"Shall I bring to the time of birth, and not cause
delivery?" says the Lord. "Shall I who cause delivery
shut up the womb?" says your God.
—*Isaiah 66:9*

A Barren Church

The lighting in the huge church auditorium was dim. The carpet had
an "old house" smell to it—not bad, just old. The pews were beautiful, but well worn. Everything was clean and orderly. This was a
church I had wanted to visit for several years; I had heard so much
about the previous pastors, the sermons preached here, the writings
that emanated from this place, the influence of this great church.

Finally, I was standing in the sanctuary minutes before the
service was to begin, and I was to be the speaker. My expectation
turned to sorrow as a trickle of people spread over several of the
pews. The worship was stale; "depressing" might be a better

word. The people were spiritually suffering; "dead" might be a truer word. What had happened to this great church? It had been so fruitful, but now was so barren.

Barren churches...how do they happen?

A Barren Ministry

The conversation was awkward, tense, slow, one that I desired to end quickly. The discussion of the past was even more difficult. His ministry had been one of national influence. You know the kind: a ministry that was in the speaker lineup for all the big conferences, best-selling books, popularity...all that a leader could dream of in these areas of success. *Is there a difference between success and fruitfulness?* I wondered.

As we conversed, the past was not the issue—it was the ever-darkening present. The "now" part of this pastor's life was a picture of failure and brokenness. God had allowed a stripping, a humbling to take place.

The problem, though, was that this person did not recognize the "God part"; he was annoyed at people. His focus was on everything and everyone but God and himself. He blamed the leaders who worked with him, the media who ruined him, the Body of Christ that was shallow, narrow-minded, lacking in true love and loyalty.

I tried to be gracious and honest, understanding and patient. He had been so fruitful, but was now so barren. What had happened to this man, to this ministry?

How do ministries move from fruitfulness to barrenness? The more important question is, How do barren ministers, churches, movements, marriages and believers move from barrenness back to fruitfulness?

Barrenness Defined

A journey through the Old Testament Hebrew words and New Testament Greek words will enable us to grasp the biblical meaning of barrenness and help us to more accurately examine this subject. There are basically six Hebrew and two Greek words associated with the barrenness subject.

Hebrew Definitions[1]

Aqar: An adjective describing someone who has non-functioning generative organs; to be barren, whether male or female. (See Gen. 11:30; Exod. 23:26; Deut. 7:14; Judg. 13:2,3.)

Shakol: To miscarry; to suffer an abortion; by analogy to bereave; literally and figuratively; to be childless; to be robbed of children. The Hebrew word is translated to be bereaved, to miscarry, to rob, to destroy, to be childless, to be empty, to fail to bear fruit, to cast her fruit before the time. (See Gen. 27:45; Exod. 23:26; Lev. 26:22; Deut. 32:25.)

Melechah: A salted land; a desert barren land; no produce; no life; dead to seed. (See Job 39:6; Ps. 107:34; Jer. 17:6.)

Otser: To restrain, enclose; by analogy to hold back; to constrain; to close up; detain; refrain; shut up. (See Ps. 107:39; Prov. 30:16; Isa. 53:8.)

Shakkuwl: Derived from shakol. An adjective describing being robbed of children; deprived; attacked; taken advantage of. (See 2 Sam. 17:8; Prov. 17:12; Song of Sol. 4:2; Jer. 18:21; Hos. 13:8).

Tsiyah: Literally, a parched land; a desert; a land under drought; a solitary place; a wilderness.(See Ps. 63:1; Isa. 41:18; Jer. 51:43; Ezek. 19:13.)

Greek Definitions[2]

Steiras: A contraction; stiff and unnatural; sterile. (See Luke 1:7,36; 23:29; Gal. 4:27.)

Argos: An adjective meaning inactive; unemployed; lazy; useless; idle; slow; barren. (See Matt. 12:36; 1 Tim. 5:13; Titus 1:12; Jas. 2:20; 2 Pet. 1:8).

Dictionary Definition

Nonproductive; not functioning properly; empty; not conceiving or producing at all or only in very small quantities. Unfruitful, sterile, not fertile, not producing the usual fruit, not copious, scanty, dull, uninventive. The quality of not producing its kind, want of the power of conception.[3]

Perhaps this definition describes your ministry or the church where you are ministering right now. Maybe it's not your fault; maybe you've inherited a barren church that is nonproductive and certainly doesn't function according to your desires or

☻

Your barrenness could be a much greater sign of future success than you might imagine.

☻

God's. You may be very discouraged, very frustrated or feeling very condemned regarding your church or your ministry. You may question if you will ever experience spiritual prosperity, fruitfulness or some level of satisfaction. You may be asking, "Is there any formula for moving a church from barrenness back into the plans and purposes of God?"

The answer is an absolute yes, yes, yes! God is not finished with you, your ministry or your church. God has the sacred and secret keys to unlocking your barrenness.

Barrenness, the Key to Future Success

Among Semitic and Oriental peoples, generally barrenness was a woman's and a family's greatest curse. It is significant that the mothers of the Hebrew race—Sarah, Rebekah, Leah and Rachel—were all barren and sterile at one time, but by God's special intervention became fruitful.

Your barrenness could be a much greater sign of future success than you might imagine. Barrenness is used by God to work into us those spiritual virtues that are hard to embrace otherwise. Barrenness is God's secret school of success. Brokenness and barrenness are in the same family, and together produce quite a healthy offering: humility, faith, patience and hope (see Prov. 15:33; Jas. 1:2-4).

We usually don't ask for brokenness or barrenness, but God in His infinite wisdom sees to it that we go through what is necessary. As Dr. Charles Stanley has so eloquently said:

> We all know what it means to be broken—to be shattered, to feel as if our entire world has fallen apart, or perhaps blown apart. We all have times in our lives when we don't want to raise our heads off the pillow, and when we feel certain the tears will never stop flowing. Brokenness is often accompanied by emptiness—a void that cannot be filled, a sorrow that cannot be comforted, a wound for which there is no balm.[4]

When My Field Is Barren

Barrenness will pass. Barrenness will not be your portion for the rest of your spiritual journey. You may at this time feel very empty, very ignored by God and His blessings. You may look around and see others in a state of spiritual bliss and wonder, *Why them; why not me?*

In times of spiritual awakening there are those who seem to receive without asking, to have revival without any real sacrifice. They are blessed, so blessed. And then there are the not so blessed...the forgotten...the lonely...the ministries and churches that watch the train go by without ever having the opportunity to get on. Am I describing your church, your ministry?

The spiritual rain is falling; the fields on all sides are yielding fruit, all but my field. What an empty feeling. Who do you talk to? What do you say? When asked how your church is doing in the mighty '90s, you want desperately to answer, "We are experiencing a level of spiritual bliss, a level of spiritual productivity," but reality is ever before you and thousands of others.

George Barna states that death is the usual outcome of a barren church:

> As is true in the business world, when a church experiences a period of intense hemorrhaging, death is the usual outcome. Of course, because churches are nonprofit entities whose existence requires only a name and a person or two to maintain the legacy, a dead church is not necessarily an ex-church. Thousands of churches across America have deteriorated to the point where they are a ministry in theory only, a shell of what they had once been. In these churches, little, if any, outreach or inreach takes place. The name and buildings may insinuate a church is present, but lives are not touched in a significant, spiritual way by such artifacts.[5]

Profile of a Barren Church

No spiritual fruit, or very little, and the little fruit takes a lot of work.

No numerical growth, except for a few transplants from neighboring churches.

No new leadership growth, no new Timothys coming up through the ranks.

No new missionary vision, no missions fever, and it's a grind to raise the money.

No real financial growth over the last several years; we're holding our own.

No real spiritual penetration into our immediate area, region or state.

No new faith challenges, no rising of faith level; it's business as usual.

No enlarging inspiring vision or mission momentum, feelings of stagnation.

No changes, no flexibility, and we seem more rigid then ever, fixed, afraid of anything new.

No new evangelism ideas, no breakthroughs, no new converts; matter of fact we're even losing some of our old membership.

No new mountains to climb, not even a hill to excite us, and even a slight step upward is a trial.

No intense fasting and prayer, not even a decent attendance at a low-intensity prayer meeting.

No free-flowing, heartfelt, God-exalting worship; even the great songs don't move us the way they used to, and new songs irritate us.

Eerily, the words from a political mystery novel I had once enjoyed came to mind, "Sir, something has gone terribly wrong. We don't know what the problem is, but we know that something has gone terribly wrong. Things aren't working out as expected."[6]

This was George Barna's response after receiving all the research data concerning today's pastors and today's churches in America. Barna goes on to describe the condition of pastors and churches:

Many pastors, by their own admission, are neither gifted nor trained to be leaders and are frustrated with ministry. Churches often fail to objectively evaluate their ministry efforts and to react intelligently to a changing culture.[7]

My perspective on Barna from his book *Today's Pastors* is that he is not a withdrawn pessimist who is bent on painting negative pictures of today's leaders and churches. On the contrary, it seems to me that he has been willing to take a true, objective, intelligent look at the Church, and then reveal his findings honestly. Barna has simply researched the American church and found many to be barren. Barna's goal is simple:

> This book is not addressed to those readers who are determined to believe all is well within the Christian church in America. It is meant for those whose urgent prayer is that God will deliver us from ignorance, complacency and poor choices so we can nurse the church, as a community of believers bound together in love, faith and service, to health and vitality.[8]

My deepest desire is that together we will break the bands of barrenness from your ministry and the churches to which we minister. Words such as "sterile," "miscarry," "abortion," "desert," "wilderness" and "unproductive" are hardly inspiring words. But they are descriptive words taken from the Scriptures that pertain to God's chosen leaders and congregations. As we honestly face off with these words in our own ministries or churches, we have the potential of breaking the bands of barrenness and releasing a new level of life and productivity. My goal is to encourage barren leaders and churches with a proper faith perspective.

Dr. C. Peter Wagner's observation is:

> It is not uncommon, however, to find churches that are fairly normal, that are growing and that function from day to day more or less the way God designed them. Others, unfortunately, are not what they really should be, except perhaps in the most minimal way. It is not inaccurate to describe such churches as sick.[9]

Whether you describe certain churches as sick or barren, the need is the same: proper diagnosis and proper treatment. When Sharon and I could not bear children we needed diagnosis. Whose is the problem in this situation? Can it be determined accurately? Can it be treated successfully? We had many people, with so-called spiritual insight, tell us we had a problem. Of course we had a problem—no children!

But why? For how long? Would a change ever take place? We found most people ministering to us out of their emotions, their own past experiences or their anger about unanswerable circumstances in their own lives. What we needed was sound, accurate, biblical thinking on a very hidden problem: barrenness.

The focus of our next chapter will include a "spiritual history" of congregational abortions and spiritual miscarriages to use in our diagnosis and treatment of barrenness.

Lessons from the School of Barrenness

In this chapter we have discovered that:

- Barrenness is scripturally described in words that connote empty wombs—"sterility," "miscarriage," "abortion,"—and occupied tombs—"lifeless," "shut up," "solitary places."
- Barrenness need not be your portion for the rest of your spiritual journey. You can bear fruit as did the once-sterile mothers of the Hebrew race.
- "A dead church is not necessarily an ex-church." There is a formula for recovery.
- You're not the only one suffering from barrenness. Many churches and ministries in America are struggling with spiritual infertility.
- Your present barrenness has the power to birth in you a host of spiritual virtues.

((Making It Personal))

1. Before we can be healed, we must courageously admit that a problem exits. Have you defined your feelings of barrenness? If not, would you be willing to do so now?

2. Have you fallen into the blame trap? Why not check your focus right now?

3. Are you willing to put up with the embarrassment and frustration of the Holy Spirit's diagnostic testings in order to reveal the root of the problem?

Notes

1. William Wilson, *Old Testament Word Studies* (Grand Rapids: Kregel Publications, 1978), p. 29. R. Laird Harris, Gleason A. Archer, and Bruce K. Waltke, *Theological Wordbook of the Old Testament* (Chicago: Moody Press, 1980), Vol. II, p. 693.

2. W. E. Vine, Merril F. Unger and William White, Jr., *Vine's Complete Dictionary of the Old and New Testament* (Nashville: Thomas Nelson Publishers, 1984), p. 51.

3. Noah Webster, *America's Dictionary of the English Language* (San Francisco: Foundation for American Christian Education, 1928).

4. Charles Stanley, *The Blessings of Brokenness* (Grand Rapids: Zondervan, 1997), p. 9.

5. George Barna, *Turn Around Churches* (Ventura, Calif.: Regal Books, 1993), p. 22.

6. George Barna, *Today's Pastors* (Ventura, Calif.: Regal Books, 1993), p. 13.

7. Ibid., p. 14.

8. Ibid., p. 23.

9. Dr. C. Peter Wagner, *The Healthy Church* (Ventura, Calif.: Regal Books, 1996), p. 7.

3

Congregational Spiritual Abortions and Miscarriages

○

To everything there is a season, a time for every
activity under heaven: A time to be born, and a time
to die,...a time to heal,...a time to mourn.

—*Ecclesiastes 3:1-3*

When Sharon and I started the long process of diagnostic testing, doctors began by exploring our medical histories. We were asked about previous experiences with pregnancy. In much the same way, diagnosis in church barrenness should begin with a "spiritual history." The first two questions that must be asked are:

1. Has there been a spiritual abortion?
2. Has there been a spiritual miscarriage?

Congregations in Crisis: Spiritual Abortion

In a figurative sense, a spiritual or congregational abortion is any fruit or produce that does not come to maturity because it has been forced into a premature birthing process; anything that fails in its progress because it did not wait for God's timing; failure to produce the intended effect because of willful disobedience to God's plan. A great thing at the wrong time can result in a spiritual abortion.

☻

A church that has conceived with a visionary leader who has had a level of success and then experienced abortion is much harder to repair than an unsuccessful church.

☻

Spiritual abortions leave scars on the congregation. A church that has conceived with a visionary leader who has had a level of success and then experienced abortion is much harder to repair than an unsuccessful church. When the church's vision has experienced life and then—through poor leadership, poor decisions, unwise budgeting or moral failure—been aborted, deep emotional and spiritual disillusionment can result. It takes special ministry to understand the abortion process and to bring healing to the church before any more vision can be cast.

A season of time must be invested in the recovery process to replenish the Body, not more talk of having children. More vision won't heal a barren church that is suffering from post-abortion emotions. A church that has experienced an abortion of vision, growth, health, leadership or momentum could have the following reactions:

• Discomfort with other churches that grow and become fruitful or successful;

- Decreased ability to experience emotions of joy, expectation or peace;
- Increased perceptions and feelings of being victimized;
- Increased and deepened feelings of low self-worth and insecurity;
- An ever-growing fear of embarrassment that others will learn of the abortion and resulting sense of failure;
- A roller-coaster-type emotional life flooded with feelings of guilt, anger and depression;
- A seasonal strong sense of regret, grief, sadness or loss with no possible way to restore or regain life again.

The Death of a Vision: Congregational Miscarriage

Miscarriage is defined as an unfortunate, unforeseen termination of an undertaking; to fail or suffer defeat, applied to persons, undertakings and things. Spiritual miscarriages, unfortunately, are a common problem among churches today.

The church may go through great trials and take much time to become pregnant with the purposes of God, the vision and the promise of the future. Therefore, when a church experiences the joy of conception, but doesn't carry anything full-term, resentment, fear and even bitterness may infiltrate the congregation. The emotional and spiritual signs of a miscarrying congregation could be numerous:

- *Inescapable sorrow:* A feeling that the church has lost something precious and is grieving deeply for it. The emotions of grief may come in waves, starting strong and then subsiding, then becoming strong again without any warning or any reason.
- *Misplaced guilt:* This kind of guilt comes because the church may feel responsible, even though it could not have stopped the miscarriage. The overriding guilt complex can cause the church to respond negatively to

a perfectly positive message or emphasis from the pul
pit. Misplaced guilt may hinder a spontaneous flow of
joyful worship or expression in the areas of corporate
prayer. The heavy atmosphere is not demonic or a
reflection of a hard-hearted people, it is simply
reflective of a church that is overburdened with unre-
solved guilt. Godly guilt comes as a result of the con-
victing power of the Holy Spirit spot-lighting sin in our
lives. It is specific, urges repentance and instructs us
into positive activities in order to prevent us from
missing the mark in the future. False guilt finds its root
in the accuser of the brethren.

- *Unending search for answers:* "But why" responses are
  common among church leaders who tend to want
  answers for spiritual miscarriages. A leader will commonly go to great lengths to pinpoint the reason for
  the failure. The search through conferences, seminars
  and books can be endless for some leaders. When
  these concrete teachings and writings don't meet the
  searcher's need, that person may turn to other more
  subjective-type sources, such as seeking out people
  with prophetic giftings, intercessors and other ministries that move in the Holy Spirit realm of receiving
  and giving information. Often, however, even more
  problems can result, especially if mixed signals are
  received, such as messages that contradict each other
  or words that pinpoint certain people, church decisions or generational curses. The ensuing confusion
  can be a very unfulfilling ride for a serious and sincere
  leader who is seeking answers for a congregation that
  has simply experienced spiritual miscarriage.

- *Obsession with church growth:* A church can feel childless when there is no real convert growth, maybe no
  growth at all, and even biological growth is slow. The
  desire for growth may then become so strong and
  intense that the "childless church" develops an absolute

obsession with the need to grow, to see souls saved and people added to the church. This obsession shrouds every other part of church life. Vision becomes muddled, blurry and obscure. Balance is almost completely forgotten; everything is for one reason: we must have children. Whatever it takes, whatever it costs—we must find a way to grow. The obsession to multiply may drive the leader to compromise biblically and with issues of integrity, and ultimately ruin the leader's credibility. The church can be led into an obsession that causes it to forget its marriage to the Lord. A marriage can still be healthy without children. Love, companionship and a destiny together can keep the marriage strong. The leader is responsible for preventing an extreme "the end justifies the means" attitude, yet the leader is to have clear plans and a strategy to accomplish desired godly results. Exercising proper leadership to position the church for healthy growth is not an obsession, it's wisdom! The leader can and should be pragmatic in ministering to a church that has experienced miscarriage. Dr. C. Peter Wagner uses the term "Christian pragmatism" or "consecrated pragmatism" in his book *Strategies for Church Growth*:

Due largely to a fear that immoral means might creep into Christian strategy, we face the widespread attitude that Christians cannot and should not be pragmatic. If pragmatic implies an "anything goes" attitude, which may harm others or offend God, I would agree. But I see the term in a different light. My dictionary defines pragmatic as concerned with practical consequences or values.[1]

The Church Leader in the Valley of Death

It takes a unique and special leader to minister to a church that has gone through or is going through a spiritual abortion or spiritual miscarriage. A church may react just like a woman reacts in the natural when these unfortunate situations have happened. And the right leadership match could make the difference between a church becoming healthy or dying. Throughout the years I've seen many leaders who were matched to a wrong congregation, at least wrong in timing.

A young pastor who has just finished his education, filled with vision, ideas and a desire to prove his leadership, should not be put into a congregation that is recovering from an abortion or miscarriage. Ministry to a congregation in this grieving state calls for some understanding of how people are feeling emotionally, spiritually and mentally. Change is the last thing people need at the onset of grief.

A church that has just experienced this kind of trauma is not excited about writing new vision statements or reworking the missions slogans. It has no interest in church-building programs, and "expansion" is not a word that pushes the buttons of its members. More staff, new staff and retrained staff all fall into the same uninspiring category.

The leader who has energy and vision and feels like he is sent to remake, reshape and revitalize a congregation that is in a state of post-trauma is in for some very disappointing reactions. The pastor may become angry with the people, frustrated with the church, pity the congregation or become personally bewildered. He may find himself asking, *Is this demonic? Is there a spiritual stronghold I can pray against and uproot? Is there sin in the church? Is it time to shut the doors and bury the church with dignity?* Unfortunately none of these questions address the real question: What has this church experienced that is hindering its right spiritual response? And how can I fix that problem?

The leader who ministers to a congregation during this season must be wise, gentle and very strategic in administering healing. The wisdom of the leader is of utmost importance. I like what George Barna says about the process of leaders bringing change to their churches:

Depending on the age and nature of a church then, the response of the pastor would necessarily be different. He might for example, caution the fast-moving church to carefully consider ramifications of what it seeks to do or may need to light a fire under the recalcitrant congregation to engage it in ministry. Each circumstance requires a different leadership strategy and set of skills. In either case, the leader must analyze and plan for proper timing of ministry attitudes.[2]

Understanding the basic causes of barrenness and how to minister specifically to a barren church will be developed throughout the following chapters. Stay tuned! Don't close the book yet; the encouragement you seek is still ahead of you. There is hope! Let's meditate on a few faith-building Scriptures:

Psalm 113:9: "He grants the barren woman a home, like a joyful mother of children. Praise the Lord!"

Isaiah 54:1: "'Sing, O barren, you who have not borne! Break forth into singing, and cry aloud, you who have not labored with child! For more are the children of the desolate than the children of the married woman,' says the Lord."

Psalm 107:35: "He turns a wilderness into pools of water, and dry land into watersprings."

Lessons from the School of Barrenness

In this chapter we have discovered that:

- A spiritual abortion or miscarriage must be followed by a season of recovery to prevent permanent emotional damage to the life of the church.
- Attempts to stimulate vision in an unhealed Body will only cause more wounding.

- Shame, regret, anger, depression and numbness must be expected and must be met with the wisdom of a seasoned, sensitive and secure leader.
- Change is the last thing people need at the onset of grief.
- The life-giving, faith-building Word of God has promises to speak into broken hearts and barren birthing chambers.

((Making It Personal))

1. Can you identify a time when you experienced a spiritual abortion or miscarriage? If so, did you allow yourself permission to recover? If not, could it be that you still have some buried pain to deal with?
2. Have you been sensitive to the pain of people in your congregation? If not, would you be willing to humble yourself and ask for their forgiveness?
3. What are some of the promises you need to anchor your faith on right now?

Notes

1. Dr. C. Peter Wagner, *Strategies for Church Growth* (Ventura, Calif.: Regal, 1989), p. 29.
2. George Barna, *Today's Pastors* (Ventura, Calif.: Regal, 1993), p. 159.

4

Discerning
the Causes of
Barrenness

☉

If any of you lacks wisdom, let him ask of God,

who gives to all liberally and without reproach,

and it will be given to him.

—James 1:5

As the doctor finished his explanation of our fertility tests, he
then began to share the results. "Well, Mr. Damazio, you should
be pleased to know that all of these tests prove that you are not
the problem."

What was this doctor thinking?

My feelings were not at all relieved! *Oh, great, it's not me. It's
Sharon, great. I suspected it was Sharon all along. Now, what
shall we do about her?* Of course, this was *not* my conclusion!

We still had a problem and we didn't know what was causing it.
More tests were ordered. We were fed up with tests, but we wanted
to uncover the source of the problem, so we submitted. Eventually

we narrowed the causes to only a dozen or so. A word of knowledge from the Lord at this point would have been well received.

I did pray for any indication of what we ought to do to find the cause of our barrenness in order to, hopefully, fix the problem. The cause never was revealed through medical tests, which obviously pressured us to go on with life without knowing.

Barrenness: God-Allowed or Devil-Driven?

Our decision was to start a family through God's gift of adoption, which included two beautiful baby girls. I often reflect on our dilemma of barrenness and how it forced us into another mindset, another "life choice" that we would probably not have made if circumstances had been different. Where would these two precious lives be today if we had not been barren? How richly they have blessed our lives and the lives of those around them!

God did not release us from barrenness until a further work had been accomplished by His dealings and by our adoption of two predestined children. Barrenness was God's hand directing us while at the same time purifying us.

In much the same way, leaders in ministry can find themselves going through dry seasons that seem like a long, scorching journey across a never-ending desert. During these times the bands of barrenness may be tight around that leader's vision, future, fruitfulness or outreach. The Christian world has no answers and the leader is forced to move on with God while asking the question, Is this barrenness God-allowed or devil-driven?

I'm not sure you can easily determine the answer to that question every time you pass through a trial such as this, but certain biblical insights can be gained by studying the lives of chosen barren people in the Scriptures, and the Bible does have much to say about curses and blessings with regard to barrenness. For example, Proverbs 26:2 says:

Like a flitting sparrow, like a flying swallow, so a curse without cause shall not alight.

As a sparrow wanders and a swallow flies about, so an unjustified curse does not alight (*Berkeley Translation*).

Like a sparrow in its flitting, like a swallow in its flying, so a curse without cause does not alight (*NASB*).

Although not all curses are judgments of God, the curse that is a judgment of God will not come without a cause. When God pronounces a curse, it is first a denunciation of sin (see Num. 5:21,23; Deut. 29:19). Second, the curse is God's judgment on sin (see Num. 5:22,24,27; Isa. 24:6). And third, the person who is suffering the consequences of sin by the judgment of God is called a curse (see Num. 5:21,27; Jer. 29:18).[1]

As we see in the following verses, fruitfulness was considered to be the result of blessing while barrenness was viewed as a judgment of God or a withholding of blessing:

Deuteronomy 7:14: "You shall be blessed above all peoples; there shall not be a male or female barren among you or among your livestock."

Exodus 23:26: "No one shall suffer miscarriage or be barren in your land; I will fulfill the number of your days."

On the borders of Canaan, Moses set before the people life and death, the blessing and the curse:

Deuteronomy 30:19: "I call heaven and earth as witnesses today against you, that I have set before you life and death, blessing and cursing; therefore choose life, that both you and your descendants may live."

The first national act upon entering the land was to set blessings and curses in motion. The blessing would overtake the obedient and the curse would overtake the disobedient:

Deuteronomy 28:2: "And all these blessings shall come upon you and overtake you, because you obey the voice of the Lord your God."

The curse causes the heavens to become like brass. (This is not to say that the curse is the only reason the heavens become like brass.) As a matter of fact, famine in the land, drought, pestilence and barrenness were all considered to be acts of God's judgment (see Deut. 28).

The wise person who has encountered spiritual barrenness, or is leading a church through a season of barrenness, must pray for discernment when attempting to determine its cause. Scripture points to two basic reasons for barrenness. The two causes are revealed by studying many of the barren people in Scripture—barren lands, barren waters and barren churches. In the following diagram the specific people and subjects to be developed in our study are simplified and categorized. The details within each cause will be addressed as we progress through the text.

Discerning Barrenness Causes

The God-Allowed, God-Used Temporary Barrenness with a Grace Covering	Certain Acts of Rebellion, of Human Failure, Satanic Harassment and Blatant Disobedience to God Result in Consequent Barrenness
1. Sarah	1. Michal (David's wife)
2. Rebekah	2. Israel
3. Leah	3. Faulty Leadership
4. Rachel	4. Diseased River
5. Manoah's Wife	5. Satanic Harassment
6. Hannah	6. Concealed Wickedness
7. Elizabeth	7. Internal Church Problems

Discernment: Enlightened Understanding

When seeking out the causes of barrenness, we must ask for and develop spiritual discernment—the ability to perceive root causes, not just surface problems. Unless we have clear direction from the Holy Spirit, we can misinterpret circumstances, dealings of God and blatant scriptural mandates (see Isa. 55:8,9,11). Often the natural mind gets in the way, and when it does, our humanity can wound the Body of Christ. A key passage to study when seeking spiritual discernment is Ephesians 1:17,18:

> That the God of our Lord Jesus Christ, the Father of glory, may give to you the spirit of wisdom and revelation in the knowledge of Him, the eyes of your understanding being enlightened; that you may know what is the hope of His calling, what are the riches of the glory of His inheritance in the saints.

20/20 Vision: Seeing Through the Eyes of the Holy Spirit

Let's look at some Kingdom directives within this passage that show us how and what to be pursuing as we seek spiritual discernment.

Spiritual Illumination
This passages suggests that you can pray to have "the eyes of your understanding...enlightened." When you pray for spiritual illumination, you ask that the eyes of your heart be flooded with light, so that your inner man will be quickened with the spiritual powers of wisdom and vision. Spiritual illumination according to Ephesians 1:17 involves the spirit of wisdom and revelation.

Spirit of Wisdom
The Greek word for "wisdom" in this passage is *sophia*, meaning insight into deep things, an understanding, a spiritual intelligence,

broad and full understanding. When seeking the causes of barrenness and the remedies to barrenness, spiritual wisdom is a necessity (see v. 8; 3:10). The Hebrew word for "wisdom" is *chokma*, meaning sound judgment, discernment, ability to see things in a right perspective (see Exod. 28:3).

Wisdom is seeing God's principles as universal, nonoptional, nonnegotiable and the pathway to true, lasting success. Wisdom

ↄ

When seeking to discern the causes of congregational barrenness, a leader must have a biblical mind-set, not just an emotional perspective.

ↄ

equips us with the ability to see how natural inclinations are usually directly contrary to the principles of God's Word. God says in His Word, "Humble yourself and you shall be exalted.... Give and you shall receive more....Lose your life and you shall find life...."

These biblical principles are countercultural to our natural way of living and, most certainly, our carnal thinking. Wisdom is the ability to use the facts and knowledge of God's Word to come to a correct conclusion. When seeking to discern the causes of congregational barrenness, a leader must have a biblical mind-set, not just an emotional perspective. As we will see, most barrenness has a biblical remedy and necessitates wise leadership (see Col. 2:8; Jas. 1:5). Wisdom obeys the Word of God, following God-ordained principles and patterns.

The Church has changed dramatically throughout the centuries—it has become more complex and more businesslike than the Early Church we read about in the book of Acts. Today the Church is a massive organization with denominations, commissions, committees, counsels, boards and programs. It quite often functions like a business rather than a body, a factory rather than a family, and a corporation rather than a community. Some churches have become entertainment centers, giving performances to passive, unproductive churchgoers. The result is a tendency to adopt the standards and values of the world in which we serve rather than raising up the standards and values of the God for whom we serve.

What seems like fruitfulness to the natural eye could be nothing more than barrenness dressed up to look like fruitfulness. What is barrenness to man is not always barrenness to God, and what is fruitfulness, prosperity and success to man is not always the same to God (see 1 Cor. 3:9,10; Isa. 33:6; Matt. 7:24-27). Therefore, to have wisdom is to have God's mind about the matter, which can only be attained as we surrender our understanding to the power of the Holy Spirit.

Spirit of Revelation

The Greek word for "revelation" is *apocalypsis,* which means receiving the insight and discernment that the Holy Spirit brings into the mysteries of life, a receptive spirit, a capacity to understand. It is the attitude of eagerness to receive illumination, a ready spirit to grasp any mystery God might deem fit to reveal. Revelation is an activity of God, not just the human faculties at work. Revelation comes by a Holy Spirit visitation, a Holy Spirit impartation (see Matt. 16:16,17; John 9:39-41; 1 Cor. 4:3-6).

Spiritual Discernment

Discernment is spiritual perception realized through the combination of God's Spirit bearing witness with our spirit as we work in harmony with Scripture and godly principles. True spiritual wisdom will produce spiritual insights into what is false or true, whether in concepts, motives or ministries. The seat of discernment is the inner man, the heart, and it is the heart that discerns or fails to discern the works of the Lord.

While understanding is a gift of God, it does not come automatically—it requires a persistent diligence. Spiritual discernment is more than intelligence quotient; it is spiritual capacity. This is attainable by all who apply themselves to God's ways and will. Philippians 1:9 says:

> And this I pray, that your love may abound still more and more in knowledge and all discernment.

Discernment is remaining free of extremes, being able to see the whole picture, not just one side or a small part of it. It is maintaining one's spiritual equilibrium, being realistic, tolerant and serious when needed (see Prov. 1:4; 8:5; 14:15; 19:25; Heb. 5:11-14; 1 Kings 3:9).

As we apply the spirit of wisdom, revelation and discernment, our specific situation may be illuminated. The question is...

Do You Really Want to Get Well?

In John 5:6 Jesus asked the invalid man who had been sick for 38 years, "Do you want to be made well?" Keith Anderson in his book *A Church for the 21st Century* says, "The same question can be asked of sick churches. They are sick from sin, lethargy, infighting, heresy, under-nourishment, incompetence, irrelevance or any of a thousand other ecclesiastical diseases. The people of the church may actually enjoy discussing the symptoms—lack of growth, insufficient finances, too few leaders, successive short-term pastorates, and so on."[2]

The first step out of barrenness is simply a desire to get well, to become a healthy, growing, functioning church. Decision then will determine your destination. Have you made that choice? If so, let's consider the causes of barrenness by studying the chosen vessels recorded in Scripture who were tested, tried and triumphant with barrenness allowed by God. We'll also look at barrenness caused by carnal, sinful or satanically influenced acts in order to discern their roots, repent for their fruits and replant for a future harvest.

Lessons from the School of Barrenness

In this chapter we have discovered that:

- Barrenness can be God-allowed or devil-driven.
- A curse cannot land without a cause.
- Spiritual discernment reveals the root causes rather than the surface problems.
- What is barrenness to man is not always barrenness to God, and what is fruitfulness, prosperity and success to man is not always the same to God.
- True spiritual wisdom will produce spiritual insights into what is false or true, whether in concepts, motives or ministries.
- Discernment is not for the casual inquirer, it is the result of persistent diligence.
- The first step out of barrenness is simply a desire to get well, to become a healthy, growing, functioning church.

(((Making It Personal)))

1. Are you willing to allow God to expose the hidden motives of your heart, the flaws in your character and the defects in your ministry in order to break the bands of barrenness?
2. In what ways have you sought to lean on your own understanding rather than God's wisdom to discern the cause of your barrenness?
3. Are you stuck in the symptoms rather than the solutions to your barrenness?
4. Do you really want to get well?

Notes

1. William Eerdman, *The New Bible Dictionary* (Downer's Grove, Ill.: Intervarsity Press, 1982), p. 283.
2. Keith Anderson, *A Church for the 21st Century* (Minneapolis: Bethany House Publishers, 1992), p. 127.

5

Sarah: Lessons in Tested Faith

ԁ

Show the same diligence to the full assurance of
hope until the end, that you do not become sluggish,
but imitate those who through faith and
patience inherit the promises.

—*Hebrews 6:11,12*

The airport was packed and I was late for my connecting flight. I was anxious to get off the plane and race to my connecting gate. The flight attendant had asked for those not connecting to let the other passengers go first, but no one seemed to be moved by her request for mercy. Everyone packed the aisles and it was slow moving. I wouldn't normally have been that concerned, but my connection was an overseas flight and if I missed it, my whole itinerary would change.

Finally off, I raced with my carry-on bag and briefcase down the airport runway and over to the international wing. I was sweating, out of breath and very anxious. At the counter I asked, "Excuse me. Excuse me. Has flight 119 already departed?"

A smiling United worker pointed over to the reader board. The words were easy to read: DELAYED! Feeling a little embarrassed, I slipped away from the counter for a good laugh. All that worry, work and unplanned exercise, and the flight had been delayed.

When "Delayed" Does Not Spell "Relief"

This was one of those few times that "delayed" was a blessing. Usually I hate the thought of being interrupted, slowed down or stopped. The other word I cringe at is "canceled," when traveling that is. The reason is that canceled usually just means more waiting. No one really enjoys waiting, waiting in lines, waiting at doctors' offices, waiting for answers from people we've written to. Even being left on hold bothers some people!

Delay means "to cause to be late or slower than expected or desired, to go or move slowly so that progress is hindered, to put off until a later time."[1] Even the definition is unenjoyable to read. It sounds too much like life! *Roget's Thesaurus* offers more: detain, hang up, hold up, retard, set back, slow down, dally, dawdle, dilly-dally, drag, lag, linger, loiter, procrastinate, detain. Now that's putting a word into perspective!

You and I know well that life has many surprising delays, most without warning. To be delayed 15 minutes is tolerable; after an hour we're ready to cry "unjust"; a day or more is a nightmare to share with your grandchildren later in life! What would you do with 39 years of delays? 39 years of waiting? 39 years of barrenness?

Genesis 11:30 simply reads, "But Sarai was barren; she had no child." Genesis 21:1,2 says, "And the Lord visited Sarah as He had said, and the Lord did for Sarah as He had spoken. For Sarah conceived and bore Abraham a son in his old age, at the set time of which God had spoken."

Permit me to illustrate this in chart form so we can grasp the time line in the life of Sarah, the barren woman, and Abraham, the father of all who believe.

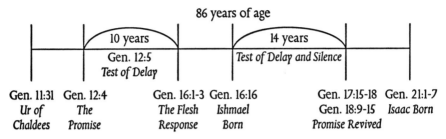

Romans 4:19 sheds light on how their barrenness was handled and remedied:

> And not being weak in faith, he [Abraham] did not consider his own body, already dead (since he was about a hundred years old), and the deadness of Sarah's womb.

Out of natural impossibility, the deadness of both Sarah and Abraham, we see the supernatural overshadowing their circumstances to bring life out of death. Where there was barrenness, no hope, no possibility, no natural resources, God gave a miracle of faith.

Refining and Refiring Faith in the Furnace of Life

The life of Abraham and Sarah was a life in the school of barrenness. The lessons they learned were not mastered in a classroom, but in the furnace of life. Abraham and Sarah's faith struggles are recorded in Scripture to encourage all who believe and will learn to walk uprightly during seasons of delay, silence and barrenness. The life of faith is built around *promises given, tests encountered* and *fulfillment enjoyed.* For every promise, there is a test, and with every test there is grace, mercy and the strength of the Almighty to see us through (see Ps. 105:19).

Barren Sarah and barren Abraham received clear promises, indicating what God would do for them in their barren condition. Both responded, but their responses lacked the one and only element that could deliver them from their barrenness—faith.

Their first response was in the realm of reasoning rather than faith. When we speak of reasoning, we mean "the cause, ground, principle or motion of anything said or done; that which supports or justifies a determination, plan or measure; a faculty of the mind by which man distinguishes truth, determines what is right and devises opinions and makes decisions from his reasonings."[2]

To reason correctly is to infer from propositions that are known, admitted or evident to a natural conclusion. However, people may reason wrongly as well as rightly. Abraham and Sarah had to go through—as do all who receive a vision, word or promise from God—the reasoning test.

The Reasoning Test

As with most tests, the reasoning test has multiple-choice solutions that are often masked in partial truths and then complicated by human error. Let's look at some of them.

Religious Reasoning

Genesis 16:2 says, "Now behold, the Lord has prevented me from bearing children" (*NASB*). This reasoning was partially right and partially wrong. But the partial truth that Sarah walked in became the basis for a spiritual error. The Lord had not prevented her from having children *forever*. The delay was not a conclusion to the matter. It was a case of divine timing. Religious reasoning caused Sarah to take the matter into her own hands and to devise a plan for fulfilling God's promise. Sarah reasoned and rejected the faith-miracle factor that God could—in her state of barrenness, at His choosing—give her a child. She instead concocted a plan, using her handmaid, Hagar, to produce a child named Ishmael, who would fulfill God's promise. The problem: God will not honor our religious remedies.

Good Source Reasoning

Genesis 16:2 tells us, "And Abraham listened to the voice of Sarai" (*NASB*). Sarah had an influential voice in this matter. She was the suffering, barren woman. She was the beloved wife of Abraham. The sound of her voice brought a sense of assurance and security. Surely God would honor what this suffering, frustrated and humble woman of God was desiring. Her plan had earmarks of something God could use to put a stop to all of this delay business. Besides, God had been silent concerning the issue. It was now Sarah and Abraham's responsibility to carry on the vision. This wrong reasoning would hinder the plans and purposes of God, and birth an Ishmael whose offspring would be a thorn in Israel's side for generations to come. God had not been the initiator of Sarah's idea and would not use Ishmael to fulfill His promise.

Natural Instinct Reasoning

Genesis 16:1-3 shows that after 10 years in Canaan, Sarah was still barren. The promise was still unfulfilled. Sarah in her "natural instinct" reasoning simply suggested that they take matters into their own hands. The carnal mind always seeks to aid God's working. Unbelief is prolific with creative schemes. There was no human hope that the promise could be accomplished in the form in which they had first understood it. And yet it is always hard to resist the temptation to bow to natural reasoning, especially when it appeals to natural instincts.

Cultural Reasoning

Genesis 16:1 states, "And she had an Egyptian maidservant whose name was Hagar." Sarah had within her household an answer to her problem. What Sarah proposed was a very common practice in those days. Ancient tablets containing marriage contracts discovered by archaeologists specify that a barren woman was required to provide a woman for her husband for the purpose of procreation. This idea was not sinful in and of itself. It was an acceptable cultural practice to handle what seemingly could not be changed—barrenness. Abraham had allowed thought patterns and practices which he had learned from his pagan culture to influence his thinking. But God wanted Abraham and Sarah to use faith, the "God answer" in their circumstance, not Hagar, the "cultural answer."

The Challenge Never Changes:
Trust and Obey

The modern-day barren church or ministry experiences all of the same problems Sarah and Abraham had to face, embrace and surrender to God for a remedy. Leaders will encounter the reasoning test during times of vision delay and a "God silence" to work deeply in their ministries.

What is challenged? Our ability to trust God's Word, God's ways and God's simplicity, which is at times mind-boggling, in methods of building His Church. Religious reasoning, good source reasoning, natural instinct reasoning and cultural reasoning may be some of the greatest obstacles we leaders will face before seeing God move mightily in our ministries and churches.

Barrenness reflects the lack of God's obvious blessing. Broken bands of barrenness will be accompanied by a canopy of grace: people being added to the church daily, financial release, multiplication in the leadership, increased missions activity, city penetration, family restoration and healthy signs of spiritual life.

At times it is easier to follow our natural inclination and cultural wisdom and to use the resources available to bring the blessing we so desperately desire. We may yield to methodology, managerial paradigms and leading-edge concepts for our numerical growth. These are not sinful in and of themselves, but without faith (the spiritual element that God responds to), all of these things are Ishmaels. Romans 14:23 tells us that "whatever is not from faith is sin." Buildings, programs, ideas, creative evangelism, seeker-sensitive innovation may all fall into the Ishmael category.

Joseph Stowell states this fact quite eloquently in his book *Shepherding the Church into the Twenty-First Century:*

Unfortunately, hitting the mark these days is tougher than it's ever been. The dramatic shift of our society has tended to blur vision and divide our focus. The shift is disoriented and has discounted the quality of the flock as well. Some have assumed that this new environment demands new targets, targets more related to programmatic configuration that address the cultural change, therapeutic perspectives that address the fallout in personal lives. Our fault is not that we are asking how to do church in this new and challenging context or that we are wrestling with how we heal the phenomenal brokenness that increases around us. Our fault is that we are tempted to assume that this new environment changes the target, while our new environment has simply changed the direction and velocity of the wind.[3]

The cultural context is both challenging and a source of leadership temptation. We are to minister within our culture, but not allow cultural fads, methods or philosophy to replace the simplicity of our faith in God's Word and God's power. The Spirit of God is well able to build great churches and fruitful ministries.

The Promise Revived, Revisited and Recovered

Sarah's bands of barrenness were broken by one visitation *of God.* Genesis 21:1,2 says that "the Lord *visited* Sarah as He had said, and the Lord did for Sarah as He had spoken. For Sarah conceived and bore Abraham a son in his old age, at the set time of which God had spoken" (italics added).

Our churches will change as we receive our visitation of God's holy presence upon our brokenness, our barrenness and our human failures. God will visit us according to His promises. He will do for us according to His Word. It will be in His timing, not ours. It will be through His miracle power, not our slick managerial leadership styles.

The visitation from God upon a barren person is the visitation of His Holy Spirit, His fresh and powerful presence. The Scriptures speak of a reviving or a refreshing promised to the Church. The most common Old Testament word translated "revive" comes from the Hebrew verb *hayah,* which in one sense means "to be" but in another sense means to recover, repair, give new life, refresh, restore and to make alive again. *Webster's Dictionary* defines revival as "return, recall or recovery to life from death or apparent death; bringing something back to life that is either now dead or seemingly dead; renew the mind or memory, to recover from a state of neglect or depression, to awaken, reinvestigate."

J. Edwin Orr said, "Spiritual awakening is a movement of the Holy Spirit bringing about a revival of New Testament Christianity in the church of Christ and its related community."[4] According to Stephen Olford, "Revival is the sovereign act of God in which He restores His own backsliding people to repentance, faith and obedience."[5] A favorite among revivalist researchers is Charles Finney, the great revivalist during the Great Awakening of the 1700s. He says, "Revival presupposes that the church is sunk down in a backslidden state, and revival consists in the return of the church from her backslidings and reaping the harvest of souls."[6]

His Visitations, Our Preparations

Past visitations may not be indicative of future visitations. God could be up to something new. We may miss a new visitation of God if we are:

- Not open to accept the Holy Spirit moving in a fresh way because it is not according to our denominational or religious background.
- Not open, because the new way is illogical to the natural mind.
- Not moving in fresh truths because of fear that we may be identified with those who have misused or abused these same truths.

A visitation of God today upon the church:

- May only come to those who have prepared for visitation and are prayerfully anticipating it;

- May be more of a slow "adding" to the church by God's presence than by a "revival" type outpouring that comes quickly and subsides;
- May mean a cleaning up of His house, a "sweeping clean visitation," which is not popular but probable;
- May be an overwhelming sense of God's approval by His presence to those who are building by God's principles and patterns.

Psalm 65:9-13 yields eight descriptions of God's visitation:

A time of spiritual watering by the rain of God;
A time of enriching river;
A time of spiritual provision;
A time of soil preparation;
A time of blessing and prosperity;
A time of global ministry;
A time of sheep multiplication;
A time of rejoicing.

Faith It Till You Make It

Sarah's bands of barrenness were broken by believing in the promise. "And the Lord visited Sarah as He had said" (Gen. 21:1). It will be our believing in God's Word or promise by faith, not by the natural mind, that will break our barrenness.

Romans 4:20 says, "He staggered not at the promise of God through unbelief; but was strong in faith, giving glory to God" (*KJV*). Abraham did not "stagger" or "waver through unbelief." He rejected unbelief and remained faithful to God's promise. Unbelief, doubt and staggering are all products of a barren heart (see Ps. 78:19; 2 Kings 7:2).

The word "stagger" again points us toward the problem of leaning on our reasoning tendencies. To stagger means to make use of our own judgments and rationale in discerning things. To "stagger at the promise" is to take into consideration the promise and all the difficulties that lie in the way of its accomplishment and to dispute its fulfillment. Staggering is not to fully cast it off nor to fully embrace it, but to waver over it.

The Promise	The Decision	The Problems
Seems incredible	Stagger, waver, doubt	No natural way
Seems beyond us	Or	No tangible evidence
Seems impossible	Trust, faith, believe	No right circumstance

Unbelief focuses on our power to accomplish, fulfill and make things happen. But depending upon our own limited resources only magnifies the problem. Unbelief is also strengthened when

☻

The more difficult the fulfillment [of the promise], the more powerful and wonderful will be our matured faith. Faith grows by going through the test, the seasons of delay and silence.

☻

we focus on the natural, physical and temporal things of life. Giving all our attention to circumstances without a faith attitude will discourage our souls. Instead, when God promises something, we must magnify His power and refer the event to His will.

The more difficult the fulfillment, the more powerful and wonderful will be our matured faith. Faith grows by going through the test, the seasons of delay and silence.

Strong faith is not antirational—it is supported by abundant reasons. All the reasons that justify our believing in God at all justify our believing in Him most firmly. He cannot lie! He is all powerful! He is God! Is anything too hard for the Lord? By having unquestioning confidence in His promises, we bring glory to God and break the bands of barrenness.

Often we are brought to the end of our resources and go to

pieces, like Paul's ship. Yet at the right time and in the right way, the divine Promiser fulfills His promise; the fulfillment is as certain as His own existence (see Heb. 1:3,14; 11:2; Rom. 4:20).

Just as Abraham and Sarah broke the bands of barrenness by exercising faith in God who always fulfills His word, so our faith can grow strong when the winds of adversity blow the hardest. Faith and patience inherit the promises of God. Let's face it! The promise will not be fulfilled without problems. Therefore you must decide now: "I will not stagger. I will not give up. I will wait for the promise."

Our attitude must be steadfast. We must have a disposition of mind that will accept the adversities and the crosses disposed to us by providence.

The Faith Attitude

A faith attitude is:

- A thorough persuasion that nothing befalls us by fate or by chance or by the mere agency of inferior causes, but that all things proceed from the dispensation of or with the allowance of God (see Job 2:10);
- A firm belief that all occurrences, however adverse and cross to our desires, are well consistent with the justice, wisdom and goodness of God (see Job 38:1—42:6);
- A full satisfaction of mind that all things, even the most bitter and sad accidents, do work together for our good according to God's purpose (see Gen. 45:5; 50:20,24; Rom. 8:28);
- An entire submission and resignation of our wills to the will of God, suppressing all rebellious insurrections and grievous resentments of heart against His providence (see Matt. 26:36);
- Bearing adversities calmly, cheerfully and courageously in order to avoid being discomposed with anger or grief; not to be put out of humor, not to be dejected or

disheartened, but in our disposition of mind to resemble the New Testament saints who "took joyfully the spoiling of [their] goods" (Heb. 10:34, *KJV*), and who counted it all joy when they fell into various tribulations (see Jas. 1:2);

- A hopeful confidence in God for the removal or easement of our afflictions and for His gracious aid to support us well, living according to these precepts: "It is good that one should hope and wait quietly for the salvation [provision] of the Lord" (Lam. 3:26). "Rest in the Lord, and wait patiently for Him" (Ps. 37:7). "Wait on the Lord; be of good courage, and He shall strengthen your heart" (Ps. 27:14);

- A willingness to continue, during God's pleasure, in our afflicted state without weariness or irksome longings for alteration;

- Humility of mind wrought by our adversity, which softens our hard hearts. Humility or lowliness means to be sober in our self-understanding, sensible of our manifold defects and sins. It includes being meek and gentle, tender and pliable in our temper and frame of spirit, deeply affected with reverence and dread toward the awful majesty, mighty power, perfect justice and complete holiness of God.

Faith in God as the Promiser

The following are some verses that are important to rest your faith upon when walking through seasons of barrenness:

Numbers 23:19: "God is not a man, that He should lie, nor a son of man, that He should repent. Has He said, and will He not do it? Or has He spoken, and will He not make it good?"

1 Kings 8:56: "Blessed be the Lord, who has given rest to His

people Israel, according to all that He promised. There has not failed one word of all His good promise, which He promised through His servant Moses."

Psalm 84:11 "For the Lord God is a sun and shield; the Lord will give grace and glory; no good thing will He withhold from those who walk uprightly."

Isaiah 55:10,11: "For as the rain comes down, and the snow from heaven, and do not return there, but water the earth, and make it bring forth and bud, that it may give seed to the sower and bread to the eater, so shall My word be that goes forth from My mouth; it shall not return to Me void, but it shall accomplish what I please, and it shall prosper in the thing for which I sent it."

Hebrews 6:18: "That by two immutable things, in which it is impossible for God to lie, we might have strong consolation, who have fled for refuge to lay hold of the hope set before us."

Hebrews 10:23: "Let us hold fast the confession of our hope without wavering, for He who promised is faithful."

Lessons from the School of Barrenness

In this chapter we have discovered that:

- The life of faith is built around promises given, tests encountered and fulfillment enjoyed.
- We must all face the reasoning test as we pass through seasons of barrenness.
- Partial truths are usually the basis for spiritual error.
- When we try to birth answers to God's promises, we find ourselves living with Ishmaels that mock our promises and make us miserable.

- Unbelief is prolific with creative schemes that delay the promise, deepen our depression and derail our focus.

((Making It Personal))

1. If you are experiencing barrenness, you have probably encountered the reasoning test. In what ways have you tried to "help" God fulfill His promise?
2. Have your efforts birthed any Ishmaels that now mock your faith and make you feel embarrassed or angry? Rather than blaming your Ishmael, what have you learned about yourself through this test?
3. Where is your focus? Are you fully convinced that God is who He says He is?
4. Will you take the challenge to memorize the verses at the end of this chapter so your faith will be anchored upon His Word?

Notes

1. *Webster's New Twentieth Century Dictionary—2nd Edition*, (U.S.A.: Collins World Publishers, 1978), p. 479.
2. Ibid.
3. Joseph Stowell, *Shepherding the Church into the Twenty-First Century* (Colorado Springs: Victor Books, 1994), p. 12.
4. Winkie Pratney, *Revival Principles to Change the World* (Pittsburg, Pa.: Whitaker House, 1983), p. 16.
5. Steven F. Olford, *Lord Open the Heavens* (Grand Rapids: Harold Shaw Publishers, 1980), p. 26.
6. Charles Finney, *Revivals of Religion* (Grand Rapids: Fleming H. Revel, 1962), p. 7

6

Rebekah: Lessons in Contradictions and Intercession

⌣

And the Lord restored Job's losses when he prayed
for his friends. Indeed the Lord gave Job twice as
much as he had before.

—*Job 42:10*

Pray for barren women?! My wife had been barren for several
years. I had fasted, prayed, wept, laughed, threatened, bargained,
and nothing had happened. So when the Holy Spirit first asked
me to move in the realm of faith for something I had no apparent success in, I'm embarrassed to reveal that my response was
much like Jonah's—I didn't want to obey.

Months later, when I heard the news that several women had
what they called "miracle babies," I was murmuring, grumbling
and discouraged. I wanted to find my juniper tree and call it
quits. This was hardly a proper response to someone's special
miracle!

The Contradiction Test

Contradiction. The word ruminated in my mind. For out of my barrenness others had been blessed with fruitfulness. Out of my brokenness others received wholeness. Out of my weakness others had received strength. Slowly but surely, this spiritual law of contradiction that had been in the shadows of obscurity was beginning to take on clarity. I began to see it in Scripture—first through Jesus' life, then in the lives of other biblical characters. Jesus endured contradictions with joy, stayed on course and finished His race. Hebrews 12:3 reads, "For consider him that endured such *contradiction* of sinners against himself" (*KJV* italics added).

To contradict is to assert the opposite of what someone has said, to speak in denial, to have someone oppose you. A contradiction is when things tend to be contrary to each other, a thing containing contradictory elements. Chuck Swindoll speaks of contradictions with rare insight:

What a strange lot we are! Enamored of the dazzling lights, the fickle applause of the public, the splash of success, we seldom trace the lines that led to that flimsy and fleeting pinnacle. Bitter hardship. Unfair and undeserved abuses. Loneliness and loss. Humiliating failures. Debilitating disappointments. Agony beyond comprehension suffered in the valley and crevices of the climb from bottom to top.[1]

Most of God's servants who received a promise, vision, dream or faith direction were tested and challenged with contradictions. Let's look at a few of them:

- Abraham and Sarah received the promise of a miracle son, but she was barren.
- Joseph dreamed of promotion and prosperity but received prison and hatred.

- Moses received a word that he would be a deliverer but was rejected and sent into the wilderness.
- David was anointed to be king but was driven into hiding by the jealousy of King Saul.
- Stephen was stoned and died. Paul was stoned and lived.
- Philip was supernaturally transported, but Paul was shipwrecked and snakebitten.
- Peter walked on water. Paul floated in the water for three days.
- James was beheaded while Peter was released.

The Cross: When Our Wills Cross God's Will

Contradictions in life and ministry are numerous and part of God's sovereign school of shaping great leaders. Contradictions are our crosses to bear, and we are commanded to bear them (see Matt. 16:24). A cross is made of two pieces of wood meeting and crossing each other, running contrary to each other. As we've often heard, the cross represents our thoughts crossing God's

☻

God sends contradictions to test our responses or reactions. Will we become broken or bitter? Soft or hard?

☻

thoughts, our will crossing God's will, our desired results or answers crossing God's given answers.

God allows contradictions to enter our perfect worlds to press us, break us and bring us to our knees. God sends contradictions to test our responses or reactions. Will we become broken or bitter? Soft or hard? Our confession changes as we embrace contradictions or the unchangeable circumstances of life: a child born with mental or physical problems; a disease that refuses to let go of a friend or loved one; an accident that takes the innocent godly person into eternity at the height of his or her life and ministry; a church that splits right after a vision meeting; a church that grows numerically, financially and in other ways while the senior pastor is living in gross sin; at the same time a pastor with utmost integrity who plods along with few people, financial scarcity and no recognition. Contradiction.

Contradictions, afflictions, the test of all promises, dreams, visions—this is the way of the Cross. This is the way of ministry both in barren churches and in productive churches. During the contradiction test, Psalm 18:30 may be hard to confess: "As for God, His way is perfect; the word of the Lord is proven." However, once we have come through it, we can say, "Before I was afflicted I went astray, but now I keep Your word" (Ps. 119:67).

Looking back, Sharon and I realize that we didn't choose the trial of barrenness, nor could we have dictated the time of its ending. God had His perfect way because we had no choice. We wanted God's best so we submitted to His test. His Word is true (see Ps. 12:6).

As pastors and leaders, we identify with the trial of barrenness because we all go through it during different seasons of our church, ministry and personal lives. And when we go through it, what we desire simply does not happen at all or happens so slowly that we become totally discouraged. Let me assure you, this is a test, only a test! Be encouraged with the barrenness you face today, with those unexplainable contradictions that loom over your life and ministry. Reinvite God into a place of fruitful activity in the face of your barrenness for "This too shall pass."

Lessons from Barren Rebekah

Rebekah, Isaac's barren wife, received a promise of unparalleled growth, which we read about in Genesis 24:60: "And they blessed Rebekah and said to her: 'Our sister, may you become the mother of thousands of ten thousands; and may your descendants possess the gates of those who hate them.'"

Rebekah received the promises of divine blessing, supernatural growth and victory in warfare. Every pastor has received the same promises in the following passages:

Matthew 16:18,19: "And I also say to you that you are Peter, and on this rock I will build My church, and the gates of Hades shall not prevail against it. And I will give you the keys of the kingdom of heaven, and whatever you bind on earth will be bound in heaven, and whatever you loose on earth will be loosed in heaven."

Matthew 28:17,18: "When they saw Him, they worshiped Him; but some doubted. And Jesus came and spoke to them, saying, 'All authority has been given to Me in heaven and on earth.'"

Luke 24:46-49: "Then He said to them, 'Thus it is written, and thus it was necessary for the Christ to suffer and to rise from the dead the third day, and that repentance and remission of sins should be preached in His name to all nations, beginning at Jerusalem. And you are witnesses of these things. Behold, I send the Promise of My Father upon you; but tarry in the city of Jerusalem until you are endued with power from on high.'"

With these promises, the test of barrenness is certain. Times and seasons will arise when all you do is blanketed with barrenness rather than growth and prosperity. As leaders, pastors and spiritual mentors, our response must be an Isaac response: "Now Isaac pleaded with the Lord for his wife, because she was barren; and the Lord granted his plea, and Rebekah his wife conceived." Hold your promise before the Lord for your particular ministry, flock, congregation or group. "Holding up the promise" speaks of intercessory prayer.

The Three Promises to the Barren Church

Let's consider the three promises of Genesis 24:60.

1. The Promise of Divine Blessing

And they blessed Rebekah.

The Hebrew verb "to bless" (*barak*) means "to endue with power for success, prosperity, longevity, provision, protection, glory, honor and favor."[2] These words speak of success in everything you put your hand to do, to be raised to great honor and receive promotion (see Gen. 39:3,23; Josh. 1:7; Ps. 1:3; 118:25; 122:7; 2 Chron. 26:5; 31:21).

The true blessing of God is received by those who *trust* God and *abide* by His principles without manipulating those principles. They trust that God will give what is right and leave the timing and measure of success entirely in His hands (see Mark 4:26-29; 1 Kings 3:5-15). Our prayer is for the blessing of the Lord to rest upon us. We have the assurance that "the blessing of the Lord brings wealth, and he adds no trouble to it" (Prov. 10:22, *NIV*), and that "all these blessings will come upon you and accompany you if you obey the Lord your God" (Deut. 28:2, *NIV*).

2. The Promise of Supernatural Growth

Our sister, may you become the mother of thousands and ten thousands.

This is a promise of enlargement of all areas of ministry and congregation, a new stretching that opens up windows of opportunity to receive the supernatural growth God has for me, my house, my ministry and place of spiritual service. Lord, we pray, enlarge our:

Habitation (see Isa. 54:2);
Vision (see 1 Chron. 4:10; Prov. 29:18);
Steps (see 2 Sam. 22:37);
Heart (see Isa. 60:5);

Borders (see Exod. 34:24);
Confession (see Ps. 32:1-3);
Chambers (see Ezek. 41:7; Prov. 24:3; 2 Cor. 4:7);
Ministry (see 2 Cor. 6:11,13; 10:15);

The Church in America is in desperate need of supernatural church-growth breakthrough. We have certainly organized, planned and worked diligently to see breakthroughs in true conversion growth. More than 5,000 nonchurch organizations, whose primary purpose is evangelism in America, are now sanctioned by the IRS. This includes some 2,000 itinerate evangelists who travel frequently, making public presentations of the gospel.[3]

3. The Promise of Victory in Warfare

And may your descendants possess the gates of those who hate them.

To possess the gates of the enemy was to occupy the place of authority, power and ultimate control. Biblically, gates represented the entrances of the ways leading to life and to destruction. The word "gates" then became a synonym for power because of the strength and importance of the gates to the city. Gates also represented those who held covenant and administered justice. Proverbs 8:34 says, "Blessed is the man who listens to me, watching daily at my gates, waiting at the posts of my doors." And in Proverbs 31:23 we read, "Her husband is known in the gates when he sits among the elders of the land." The elders, the spiritual authority of God's people, sat at the gates (see Deut. 21:19; 22:15,24; 25:7; Ruth 4:10,11).

The promise to all leaders is that the *gates* of hell shall not prevail against the Church. All the authority, power and evil influence of hell will not and cannot resist a restored church. Hell's gates shall pour out its hosts to assault the Church of Christ, but the Church shall not be overcome. Hell will fortify itself against the Church, but its gates will not hold out against the Church. Instead, the Church will batter down the gates of hell. Matthew 16:18 in other translations underscores our victory in warfare:

- "And the gates of Hades will not overcome it" (*NIV*).
- "And the powers of death will never have the power to destroy it" (*Phillips*).
- "And the gates of Hades shall not overpower it [or be strong to its detriment or hold out against it]" (*Amp.*).
- "And the gates, doors of Sheol, shall not shut up against the church" (*Lamsa*).
- "And the gates of hell shall not hold out against her" (*Berkeley*).

Rebekah, the barren woman, received this promise long before its fulfillment. In her barren state, Rebekah's future was described as blessed beyond her imagination. She would break out of her barren condition to experience divine blessing, supernatural enlargement and victory over her enemies.

The Isaac Response: Intercessory Prayer

One of the keys to breaking the bands of barrenness is the Isaac response: "[He] pleaded with the Lord" (Gen. 25:21). The verb "pleaded" (*athar*) in this verse is one of the Hebrew words used for intercession in Scripture.[4] H. C. Leupold translates this verse, "And Isaac interceded with Yahweh in behalf of his wife, for she was childless, and Yahweh granted his entreaty and Rebekah his wife conceived."[5]

It is interesting to note that Isaac is the only patriarch whose intercession is recorded up to that point in Scripture. His prayer was for this unusual moment. He was concerned with the promised seed. This is the second time the wife of one who perpetuates the line of promise was barren and the barrenness was, in God's time, remedied. In Rebekah's situation it is intercessory prayer, Isaac standing in the gap for his barren wife, that broke the bands of barrenness. Conception or the absence of conception is more directly due to the omnipotent power of the Creator than people are ready to believe.

Intercessory prayer is intensified praying, which involves three special ingredients:

1. *Identification* of the intercessor with the one who is interceded for.
2. *Agony* to feel the burden, the pain, the suffering, the need.
3. *Authority* which is the gained position of the intercessor to speak with authority that sees results.[6]

Isaac moved into gap-standing, intercessory prayer for his barren wife. This is the Ezekiel 22:30 intercession, "So I sought for a man among them who would make a wall, and stand in the gap before Me on behalf of the land, that I should not destroy it; but I found no one." In Luke 1:13 Zacharias also interceded for his barren wife, and God answered his prayers: "But the angel said to him, 'Do not be afraid, Zacharias, for your prayer is heard; and your wife Elizabeth will bear you a son, and you shall call his name John.'"

May God open our eyes to see what the holy ministry of intercession is which we, as leaders who face barrenness, may use powerfully. We have been set apart to exercise the ministry of intercession. May He give us a large and strong heart to believe the mighty influence our prayers can have so that we may echo the words of Job: "But as for me, I would seek God, and to God I would commit my cause, who does great things, and unsearchable, marvelous things without number" (Job 5:8,9).

Stop, Seek and See

The Isaac response to discouraging barrenness could be a model example for all leaders going through the barrenness seasons—it is the "stop, seek and see" model.

Stop...Busyness is not the answer.
Seek His face...Focus, not on the barrenness, but on the God who can break the bands or give you insight and grace to handle it. Wait upon His timing.
See His answers...He alone is able to fulfill His promises.

The two main Hebrew words used for seeking the Lord are (1) *darash,* meaning "to tread, to frequent, to follow hard after as a pursuer for pursuit or search, to seek, to ask, to make diligent inquiry, to desire something deeply"[7]; and (2) *baqash*, meaning "to seek to find, seek to secure, seek the face of, desire, require, or request."[8] He who desires not from the depths of his heart makes a deceptive pray-er. Intercessory prayer that breaks barren bands begins with a seeking heart.

The following are verses (italics added) to meditate upon as you *seek* His face:

Deuteronomy 4:29: "But from there you will *seek* the Lord your God, and you will find Him if you *seek* Him with all your heart and with all your soul."

1 Chronicles 16:10: "Glory in His holy name; let the hearts of those rejoice who *seek* the Lord!"

1 Chronicles 16:11: "*Seek* the Lord and His strength; *seek* His face evermore!"

1 Chronicles 22:19: "Now set your heart and your soul to *seek* the Lord your God. Therefore arise and build the sanctuary of the Lord God, to bring the ark of the covenant of the Lord and the holy articles of God into the house that is to be built for the name of the Lord."

2 Chronicles 11:16: "And after the Levites left, those from all the tribes of Israel, such as set their heart to *seek* the Lord God of Israel, came to Jerusalem to sacrifice to the Lord God of their fathers."

Job 5:8: "But as for me, I would *seek* God, and to God I would commit my cause."

Psalm 27:8: "When You said, '*Seek* My face,' my heart said to You, 'Your face, Lord, I will *seek*.'"

Daniel 9:3: "And I set my face unto the Lord God, to *seek* by prayer and supplications, with fasting, and sackcloth, and ashes" (*KJV*).

Lessons from the School of Barrenness

In this chapter we have discovered that:

- Those who receive a promise, dream, vision or faith direction can expect to encounter the contradiction test.
- God sends contradictions to test our responses and reactions. Will we become broken or bitter?
- Even in our barren state, we are promised divine blessing, supernatural growth and victory in warfare.
- If we want to be faith giants, we must do so without manipulating His principles and we must leave the timing and measure of success entirely to Him.
- Intercessory prayer requires *identification* with the one who is interceded for, *agony* to feel the burden, and *authority* in Christ.
- We must *stop* our busyness in order to *seek* His face so we can *see* His answers.

(((Making It Personal)))

1. What are some of the contradictory places you are walking through right now? Is God asking you to give out of your barrenness?
2. Who is God asking you to intercede for as you face your contradiction test?
3. Is busyness preventing you from hearing God's voice? What is your fear? Where is your focus?
4. Are you prepared to adopt God's timetable for breakthrough? Are you willing to be content with His measure of success?

Notes

1. Charles Swindoll, *Growing Strong in the Seasons of Life* (Sisters, Oreg.: Multnomah Press, 1983), p. 70.
2. Francis Brown, S. R. Driver, and Charles A. Briggs, *The Brown-Driver-Briggs Hebrew and English Lexicon: with an appendix containing the Biblical Aramaic; coded with the numbering system from Strong's Exhaustive Concordance of the Bible* (Peabody, Mass.: Hendrickson Publishers, Inc., 1996; a reprint from the 1906 edition), hereafter referenced as *BDB*, p. 138. See also R. Laird Harris, Gleason A. Archer, and Bruce K. Waltke, *Theological Wordbook of the Old Testament* (Chicago: Moody Press, 1980), hereafter referenced as *TWOT*, #285.
3. George Barna, *Evangelism That Works* (Ventura, Calif.: Regal, 1995), p. 34.
4. *BDB*, p. 801; *TWOT* #1722. Other important Hebrew verbs for the word "intercession" are *paga* (literally "to meet"), *BDB*, p. 803; *TWOT* #1731; and *palal*, *BDB*, p. 813 and *TWOT* #1776.
5. H. C. Leupold, *Exposition of Genesis* (Grand Rapids: Baker Books, 1944), Vol. II, p. 701.
6. Norman Grubb, *Rees Howells, Intercessor* (Fort Washington, Pa.: Christian Literature Crusade, 1993), p. 71.
7. *BDB*, p. 297; *TWOT* #455.
8. *BDB*, p. 134; *TWOT* #276.

7

Leah: Lessons in Unconditional Love

◑

When the Lord saw that Leah was unloved, He
opened her womb; but Rachel was barren.

—*Genesis 29:31*

Abraham encountered the barrenness test with his wife Sarah. God was directing their steps and, in the fullness of time, visited Sarah. Isaac encountered the barrenness test with his wife Rebekah and, through intercessory prayer, turned her captivity. Jacob also encountered barrenness with his wives Leah and Rachel. All three patriarchs encountered the barrenness test, and in all three situations, God moved through their barrenness to establish His covenant seed.

Leah's Lord, the God of Compassion

Leah's situation is described in Genesis 29:32 as an affliction: "So Leah conceived and bore a son, and she called his name Reuben; for she said, 'The Lord has surely looked on my affliction. Now therefore, my husband will love me.'" Leah's name may be representative of her life as a barren woman. Leah means "wearied, faint from sickness."[1] The Lord had regard for His promise and for the less loved wife of Jacob. It seems that Jacob's love for Rachel was based largely upon her physical attractiveness, leaving the unremarkable Leah in a state of rejection.

Leah had innocently become a party to a heartless fraud, thus losing Jacob's husbandly affections. Leah's barrenness affliction was remedied by the compassion of God. She bore four sons and a daughter to Jacob. The sons were Reuben, Simeon, Levi and Judah. All were significant in the history of Israel. She later maneuvered Jacob into accepting her concubine Zilpah and bore two more sons through her: Issachar and Zebulon.

The Heartless Shepherd in the Unloved Church

The lessons from barren Leah and entrepreneurial Jacob are rich and many, so we shall discipline ourselves to brevity! Leah may represent churches ministered to by leaders without deep, godly love for their churches....A deal was cut, a hiring done, a board decision made. Maybe it was the only church open at that time or a way to get through seminary, or perhaps an opportunity to gain experience. All were selfish reasons, lacking the genuine call of God and the heart of a true loving shepherd.

Most leaders do not strategically plan to be hirelings or unloving shepherds, but the enemy of our souls and the flock will take advantage of these seemingly normal procedures to bring his hideous destruction to both leader and flock. A fastidious preacher was challenged by a layman because he boasted of his qualifications. The layman said, "Why see now, without your gown you dare not preach, without your book you could not preach, without your pay you would not preach!"[2]

God will take notice of any congregation that is experiencing barrenness and a lack of love from the leadership. When a church or ministry does not produce offspring, the temptation of the leader is to refuse to deeply love the people. This lack of true pastoral/leadership compassion is felt by the congregation and will cause deep spiritual wounds. Loving the growth, numbers, finance, building and influence more than the people is a grievous and gross error. When Leah bore Simeon she declared, "Because the Lord has heard that I am unloved, He has therefore given me this son also" (Gen. 29:33).

Negativity, the Breeding Ground for Barrenness

When leaders "hate" the church, they have usually cultivated an attitude of negativity toward their city, toward their people and toward the church building itself. Negativity is a habitual bias toward grumbling, murmuring, complaining and being pessimistic about everyone and anything. The bent toward negativity usually spirals downward, affecting everyone around. People given to negativism have usually lost the spirit of joy, their sense of humor and their passion for life, family and ministry. These people are generally known as The Grouch, Mr. or Mrs. No Fun, Sour Puss or Dr. Killjoy. Make sure you don't ask for their opinions about anything!

When a pastor or leader becomes a strongly negative person, everything around that person's sphere of influence is polluted. When the church is the recipient of this attitude, the atmosphere of the church becomes unhealthy, unhappy and unproductive. A negative attitude, if not the main source, is a great contributing factor to spiritual barrenness.

The flaws become the focus in a Leah church: The church is not located in the right city. The building is inadequate; the technology is a hundred years behind; there is no parking; the lighting is poor; the pews are uncomfortable; the audio system squeals and sounds demonically harassed; the pulpit is too short and the people are not what could be called a quality congregation. The salary is nonnegotiable and painfully low. The leadership board members are all related and have been there for decades. This is not the best choice of a church.

Negative attitudes are cultivated. Initially, only the hidden thoughts of comparison with other ministries or churches are detected; then a few lighthearted comments begin to surface. Eventually an all-out negative thought pattern infected with continual negative and sarcastic comments dominates all that is said and done. It's hard to hide: You don't love them, and they don't

☻

Negativity is usually experienced by a person who has slowly lost the attitude of appreciation for not only the little things in life, but also family, ministry or church.

☻

love you. Negativity has found root in both pastor and flock. This is a spiritual stronghold that must be weeded out immediately. In order to uproot, tear down and pull out this diabolical attitude, let's look at its causes and cures:

- Negativity is best nurtured in a person who has lost the spirit of expectation for anything good to happen.
- Negativity is usually experienced by a person who has slowly lost the attitude of appreciation for not only the little things in life, but also family, ministry or church.
- Negativity is a stronghold in the mind that Satan takes advantage of, causing depression, fear, doubt and worry.
- Negativity can be defeated by developing honesty in facing the present problem, repenting for the lack of pastoral love for God's people, and publicly beginning to make statements of hope, forgiveness, expectation, faith and appreciation.
- Negativity can be defeated as we build altars of rejoicing and take time to build memories of God's goodness.

Is it possible for ministers to hate their churches and love their ministries? Is it possible for ministers to build expectations of churches because of books, seminars, magazines, internet information and other forms of communication that exalt numbers, growth and influence? Does it really surprise us that so many churches lose pastors every two to three years solely because their Leahs do not fulfill them any longer and they are searching for their Rachels?

If It's Not Unconditional, It's Not Love

As leaders, we must all learn to give unconditional love and deep compassion to the churches we serve, despite the lack of spiritual offspring. Could it be our lack of true love for our congregations is one of the bands that limits our fruitfulness? Leah thirsted for the love denied her by Jacob. Only by the sovereign grace and compassion of God was she able to find that love as God opened her womb.

Joseph M. Stowell in his book *Shepherding the Church into the Twenty-First Century* addresses the necessity of a leader loving the church:

> Love is at the heart of what it means to be a shepherd. Shepherds are caring, flock-focused individuals whose primary motivation is not the interest of self but the interest of the safety, security and satisfaction of the flock. Given this, a discussion of love in terms of the shepherd's ministry is of great importance. And it must be more than a discussion. It must lead to a commitment that transcends the circumstances of the shepherd's life or the configuration of the shepherd's congregation.[3]

The heart of true ministry is a heart of unconditional love for God and His people. The philosopher Rousseau is purported to have said, "The more I get to know people, the more I love my dog." This attitude may be the product of a few bad days with the flock, but withdrawing and becoming cynical, hardened or heart-lessly professional is unacceptable to both God and His people.

If you desire a Leah church, a church that pleads with God for productivity in order to please the husband/pastor, then lead without love and you will have it. We must love God's people without any need to be rewarded by them, without any need to find our success identity in their success or achievement (see John 3:16; Rom. 5:8).

Church history is replete with heartbreaking, tragic stories of leaders whose focus was dedicated to using and abusing the Church for the benefit of their own needs and desires. These leaders have battered the spirit of the Church, scattered people to the four corners of the earth and damaged the testimony of Christ (see Jer. 23:1-4).

Leaders must give of themselves freely and completely, with-out reserving a part for something else or being concerned about the reward for such sacrifice. Those who choose to be passionate in their love for God's people will find God rewarding them, abundantly above all that they could ever imagine, in His way and in His time. Let it not be said, "And the Lord saw that Leah was unloved." Barrenness can be turned to awesome growth through the love of God and the love of God's leaders.

Let your Leah church feel your love, your passion and your satisfaction! Purpose in your heart that the words of Jeremiah 23:4 will be spoken of you: "'I will set up shepherds over them who will feed them; and they shall fear no more, nor be dis-mayed, nor shall they be lacking,' says the Lord."

Replacing a Negative Attitude with a Mature Attitude

You can have a mature attitude. You can become the leader God wants you to be. Your attitude can help to break the bands of bar-renness. You can raise up a Kingdom standard of loving leader-ship that will bring earthly and eternal rewards. What does a mature attitude look like? It is:

- An attitude of restraining your tongue from all complaints, discontent and murmurings, all profane, harsh expressions, importing displeasure or dissatisfaction in God's dealings toward you, arguing desperation or distrust in Him.

- An attitude of blessing and praising God, declaring your hearty satisfaction in God's proceedings with you, acknowledging His wisdom, justice and goodness therein, and expressing a grateful sense thereof as wholesome and beneficial to you; maintaining this attitude in conformity to Job who, on the loss of all his comforts, did thus vent his mind: "The Lord gave, and the Lord has taken away; blessed be the name of the Lord" (Job 1:21).

- An attitude of abstaining from all irregular and unworthy courses toward the removal or redress of your crosses, choosing rather to abide quietly under their pressure than to relieve or relax yourself by any unwarrantable means.

- An attitude of fair behavior toward the instruments of your affliction—those who brought you into it or who detain you under it by withholding relief or refusing to yield the help which you might expect; having the forbearance to express any wrath or displeasure, to exercise any revenge, to retain any grudge or enmity toward those people, but rather, even on that score, bearing goodwill and showing kindness to them.

- An attitude of patience toward those who, by injurious and offensive usage, provoke you so that you (1) will not be easily, immoderately or perniciously incensed with anger toward them; (2) do not harbor any ill will, ill wishes or ill designs toward them, but truly desire their good and purpose to further it as you have ability and occasion; (3) do not execute any revenge or do any mischief to them for requital, either in word or deed.

Should a God who laid down His life for His Bride expect any less from those who are called to care for her until His return?

Lessons from the School of Barrenness

In this chapter we have discovered that:

- God takes notice of people who are experiencing a lack of love from ministry leaders.
- Lovelessness produces negativity, which can result in barrenness.
- Negativity is a habitual bias toward grumbling, murmuring, complaining and being pessimistic.
- Lack of positive expectation, heartfelt gratitude and wholehearted forgiveness are all signs of a negative attitude.
- The heart of true ministry is one of unconditional love for God and His people.
- A mature attitude is grateful in spite of loss, forgiving in spite of persecution, and patient in spite of unyielding circumstances.

(((Making It Personal)))

1. What is your real motive for ministry?
2. Are you the leader of a Leah or a Rachel? Has your ministry been the victim of a fraudulent expectation, or are you willing to sacrifice all for your Leah?
3. Is your heart "flock focused" or "reward focused"? In what ways do you need to change?
4. What are some of the negative attitudes the Holy Spirit wants to mature in you?

Notes

1. *Strong's*, #3812.
2. Ralph Turnbull, *Minister's Obstacles* (Grand Rapids: Baker Publishing, 1972—originally published by Fleming H. Revel, 1946), p. 13.
3. Joseph Stowell, *Shepherding the Church into the Twenty-First Century* (Colorado Springs: Victor Books, 1994), p. 151.

8

Rachel: Lessons in Jealousy and Sovereignty

♻

For we dare not class ourselves or compare ourselves
with those who commend themselves. But they,
measuring themselves by themselves, and comparing
themselves among themselves, are not wise.

—2 Corinthians 10:12

I don't know which is worse, feeling the undeniable emotion of envy or jealousy toward a fellow minister, or becoming the target of jealousy from other ministers. Jealousy is not an easy emotion or mind-set to admit or keep under wraps once it starts, but one conclusion is certain: Everyone deals with this subtle enemy in life, in church and in the ministry.

Jealousy comes with varying degrees of potency. A little spark of jealousy seems easily conquered when need be. It comes, it goes, and it seldom lingers: just a hot rush once in a while or a shadow of a jealous thought, a jealous daydream. Maybe it is a logical proposition of another's worth and a quick judgment of that person such as, *He doesn't deserve it. It's not fair. He is probably compromising something else in order to have that.* Jealousy may be over a golf swing, an expensive home, car, jewelry or someone's ministry or church. But make no mistake—jealousy is cruel, destructive and swift. Its embittering flame consumes character and destroys the bloom of beauty.

Anchored in the Harbor of Envy

The Holy Spirit penetrates our hearts when we least expect it and sometimes least desire it. The word impressed upon my mind was unwelcome and, I felt, unwarranted: *Envier. Frank, you are envying that ministry. You're jealous. You must give it up!*

"Envier." *I better check my dictionary and study this,* I thought. That's a safe response to a direct hit by the Holy Spirit. Let me see, envied, envier, envious, enviously, envy. An envier..."one who envies another, one who desires what another possesses and hates him because his condition is better than his own or wishes his downfall."[1] Well, that's certainly descriptive of someone driven by carnal impulses. At first I assumed the Holy Spirit was asking me to assist in bringing deliverance to other leaders bound by this spiritual disease. Then I realized, no, that's not the case—it's me! It's my spirit that has allowed an envious jealousy to take root. How could I have done that?

To be envious is to have a feeling of uneasiness around the person envied. This harbored feeling of envy is aroused when surveying the excellence, prosperity or happiness of another. You know this feeling when you are pained by the desire of possessing some superior thing that another already possesses. With envy comes other emotions: rivalry, comparison, malice, grudges and criticism. Like a baseball runner who has been trapped between bases, I was trapped. I didn't know which way to run, so I gave up, surrendered, laid down my excuses, admitted my sin and asked for cleansing.

Envy in the ministry cannot be tolerated. It has been the demise of many great leaders and the pollution of many pure wells. Envy, the pain, the uneasiness or discontent excited by the sight of another's superiority or success is accompanied by some degree of hatred or malignity and often a desire or an effort to depreciate the other person or to take pleasure in seeing that person depressed. Envy springs from pride, ambition or jealousy, mortified that another has obtained what one has a strong desire to possess (see Job 5:2; Prov. 3:31; 14:30; 23:17; 27:4; Eccles. 9:6; Acts 7:9; Rom. 1:29; Phil. 1:15; 1 Tim. 6:4; Titus 3:3; Jas. 4:5). In Scripture envy and jealousy are usually accompanied by murder, strife, deceit, malice and other ills that bring rottenness to the soul.

A Personal Taste of Jealousy

It was really quite an innocent jealousy. His church was bigger. His buildings were nicer. His location was perfect. He had the worship leader I needed, the musicians I dreamed of. The cool people in town attended his church, the wealthy, the young, the influential. He had a better radio time and a better television spot. He had the car I would like to have driven, but I was too wise and too humble! He lived where we longed to build our retirement dream home. He golfed better. Every time I got a brochure about a conference I wanted to attend, he was already attending—as the speaker!

Jealous. Envious. These two words are interchangeable—they both stem from an unhealthy need to compare. I was in the "barren" category, and he was in the "blessed and growing without any effort" category. I found myself thinking, *If only I could be successful in all the same ways, I would then be fulfilled!*

The Barren Rachel Attitude Within the Church

The words in Genesis 30:1,2 leaped off the page and right into my life experience. They mirrored my feelings exactly: "Now when Rachel saw that she bore Jacob no children, Rachel envied her sister, and said to Jacob, 'Give me children, or else I die.'"

That's it! That's my heart and my dilemma, I thought. *I have envied the Leah church for bearing children, for being fruitful, for finding and enjoying success.*

Without realizing it, my passion had become twisted: "Give me children, lest I die. Give me growth, success, influence, or else I shall die." Not die physically, but my vision, my faith, my joy, my passions would die. Without results in the ministry, surely something would have to die, so my prayer was, "Give me, lest I die."

This insatiable appetite for producing is one of the subtle traps of ministry fulfillment and success. In ministry, success can be spelled in larger attendance numbers, better programs, more popular people, bigger buildings and a sense of celebrity around the pastors. Fulfillment is perceived as one of life's choicest gifts, a major building block toward authentic ministry and authentic fruitfulness. Rachel pastors cry, "Give me fulfillment, lest I die." But as we see in Scripture, the Rachel cry of the heart would be tempered by the dealings of God. God would give to Leah four sons before He would begin to move on behalf of barren Rachel.

The barren Rachel churches may be small in number or large in number, have massive buildings, properties and moneys or be of lesser stature. Size and money are not the issue. The Rachel church is driven by the inability to reach the ultimate edge of vision.

Trapped by the Sovereignty of God

Rachel was the fourth wife of a patriarch to suffer barrenness. God was making it very apparent that human ambitions and human services were not to carry on the line of promise and furnish the desired offspring. Rachel was the favored wife of Jacob. She was beautiful in every way. She had everything a young wife could desire, everything but the blessing of children—the one thing she could not use her beauty to influence or acquire.

Rachel was trapped by the sovereignty of God's plans and purposes. Her jealousy was unacceptable, inexcusable and her impatient carnality caused harmful results. Rachel, in her angry, jealous

state, questioned the wisdom of God and demanded from Jacob
what he could not give to break the bands of barrenness. Rachel
threatened Jacob with her unreasonable demand, "Give me children, lest I die."

Jacob's response to Rachel's jealous anger is understandable:

> And Jacob's anger was aroused against Rachel, and he said,
> "Am I in the place of God, who has withheld from you the
> fruit of the womb?" (Gen. 30:2).

He knew he could not stand in God's place as the source of
divine plans, changing people, ruling over the womb of the barren or providing the miracle of conception. Jacob understood
that both fruitfulness and its absence are under the divine will
and control of—not man or woman—but God Himself.

The lessons of patience, faith, submission to God's sovereign
ways and means are offered in the barrenness stories of all four
patriarchal wives. From them, we learn that jealousy and envy
will only complicate the desired blessings of God upon our ministries and our churches. Whatever attitudes or spirit we allow to
become dominant in our lives and ministries will be passed on
to our congregations.

In his book *Pastors of Promise*, Jack Hayford states, "I saw that
whatever 'spirit' governs me at any point or practice will determine the mood, life and practice of the whole congregation. As
a result of that pivotal encounter, I learned a crucial lesson and
during my years of ministry I have noticed a general principle. It
may not explain all church problems, but I am convinced that
many conflicts within congregations are but the sad projection of
a pastor's own lack of submission to some aspect of God's will in
his own life."[2]

Barrenness and Jealousy

Out of the brokenness and the inability to change or control the
circumstances, a person may begin to envy and become deeply

jealous of other ministers or churches. Jealousy burns like fire
(see Ps. 79:5) and is the rage of man (see Prov. 6:34). Jealousy is as
cruel as the grave (see Song of Sol. 8:6). This embittering fire will
scorch all who touch it, consume character and destroy the
potential for true spiritual fruitfulness.

Barren ministers or leaders have more pull toward this fire of
jealousy, continually weighing themselves on the success scales
and found wanting. However, jealousy does not always have a
negative connotation.

The Bible describes jealousy in two ways: good and bad. The
fire that burns in the barren Rachel church or barren Jacob leaders can be the fire of God instead of the fire of jealousy. Good
jealousy is referred to in Exodus 20:5: "For I the Lord thy God am
a jealous God," and in 2 Corinthians 11:1,2 when Paul said, "Would
to God ye could bear with me a little...for I am jealous over you
with godly jealousy" (KJV). The God-kind of jealousy is a zeal of
love and of right perspective, not a self-love, but a devotion at
white heat.

Leaders must never feed on others' failures, weaknesses or
destructions. We must keep watch over our emotions and be
introspective about our motives. For example, when we hear the
praise of our envied one, do we become coldly silent? If that person is criticized, do we become secretly glad? If that person is
exalted, do we praise God for the blessing, or do we secretly
murmur, mutter and generally nurture a bad attitude for days?

Jealousy is among the most subtle and potent weapons in
Satan's arsenal. A famous fable tells of the devil crossing the
Libyan desert where he encountered a group of small fiends who
were tempting a holy hermit. They tried him with the seductions
of the flesh; they sought to sour his mind with doubt and fears;
they told him that all his austerities were worth nothing. It was
of no avail. The holy man was immovable. Then the devil stepped
forward. Addressing the imps he said, "Your methods are too
crude. Permit me for one moment. This is what I would recommend." Going to the hermit he said, "Have you heard the news?
Your brother has been made the Bishop of Alexandria." At these

words, a scowl of malignant jealousy clouded the serene face of the holy man.[3]

Have you been scowling lately? To break the bands of barrenness, Rachel had to be set free from this hellish jealousy that was ruining her life and her future. Are you receiving instruction for

◓

Jealousy distorts our personalities, ruins our characters and floods our souls with hell's torment.

◑

your barren ministry or church? Is there a Leah church or a Leah ministry that torments your soul every time you hear, see or think of it? Is there a Leah worship leader or song writer whose blessings tighten the bands of barrenness around your soul because of your jealousy? This diabolical emotion must be dealt with.

Jealousy distorts our personalities, ruins our characters and floods our souls with hell's torment. It leaves us with heavy hearts, pale and palsied, and with lean souls. The soul burning with jealousy will nurse deceptive delusions, overlook the good in other ministries, refrain from celebrating and rejoicing with others and lack the joy for living (see Jas. 3:16).

A perfect illustration of jealousy's perilous prongs has been preserved in the arena chapel in Padua, where the pioneer of fresco painting, Giotto, has given allegorical representations of the deadly vices and their opposite virtues on opposing walls. Envy is a female figure who has long, wide ears to catch every breath of rumor that may hurt a neighbor's reputation; out of her mouth issues a serpent's tongue that is swift to poison all things sweet and tender. This serpent coils back on itself and stings the eyes of the envious one to blindness and the figure stands in flames, representing the fierce fire that consumes the heart that takes pleasure in others' injuries and is made bitter by their prosperity.[4]

Barrenness and God's Sovereignty

The barren church or ministry may well look to the pastor or leader to bring about the miracles needed to loose the bands of barrenness, as we saw when Rachel cried out for relief from Jacob (see Gen. 30:1,2). Churches may hire what appears to be the perfect leader to release growth, prosperity and fulfilled vision. This may well turn into a disappointing journey for the elder board, deacon board or whatever leadership team has hired the new pastor. The problem: The new pastor is not God!

The new pastor faced with the challenge of an older, aging, traditional church may look like the messiah of new hope and future in the board meeting, but in fact is just a human being with a gift. This distortion of focus lays an enormous amount of pressure on the pastor to produce and "give us children." This is especially true when the church has been barren for 10, 20, 30 or 100 years, and the Leah church just down the street is very productive. "Give us children, lest we die!" is a passionate cry that can ignite prayer intercession or become the threat of a carnally driven, selfish motivation.

Jacob's answer to barren Rachel is the only answer we pastors may give: "I'm not standing in the place of God." There is a God in heaven who is sovereign and His ways and thoughts are higher than ours (see Isa. 55:10,11). He is the God who has wisdom and might, and He changes the times and seasons. He removes kings and raises up kings. He gives wisdom to the wise and knowledge to those who know understanding (see Dan. 2:20,21).

Our God is not seeking counsel from man and does not feel any pressure to hurry His plans and purposes. He does according to His will in the army of heaven and among the inhabitants of the earth and none can stop His hands or say to Him, what are you doing? (see Dan. 4:35). "Can I not do with you as this potter?" He asked of Israel in Jeremiah 18:6. God claimed to have the same absolute power over the nation as the potter exercised over the clay. In Isaiah 64:8 the potter is also our Father.

God is not an indulgent father who gives His children whatever they desire whenever they want it, irrespective of moral and spiritual considerations. We leaders are *not* responsible for producing the power of new life in order to break the bands of barrenness. We *are* responsible for positioning our churches and ministries in spirit, in faith, in heart attitude and with eyes focused on an awesome God. We position, God provides and produces.

And yet, we are in a hurry to vindicate our ministries and our reputations in order to bring revival or new life to our churches. We are always in a hurry to have our desires granted, but God refuses to be stampeded into premature action. Our impatience is the outcome of dealing with barren churches, barren communities and barren ministries without being soaked in intercessory prayer and a huge dose of spiritual knowledge concerning God's sovereignty.

When God chooses to allow barrenness for a season, He is working according to His perfect plans. Our frenzied reaction to God's seeming slowness is only a reaction of desire for His full knowledge and perfect control of every circumstance that arises in our lives. We may, like barren Rachel, complain in an hour of deep distress, "God, why don't you do something? I can't take any more waiting!"

We often feel as if God has left us. However, even though Rachel and Jacob could not see God standing amid the shadows, disclosing His presence and plans, He was there with His unerring hand, never losing hold of the reins. Yes, at times God seems to hide Himself (see Isa. 45:15), but God is always present, a very present help in times of trouble (see Ps. 46:1-4).

Genesis 30:22 reads, "Then God remembered Rachel, and God listened to her and opened her womb." The bands of barrenness dropped to the ground when the timing of God was perfect. God had completed a work in Rachel that no other test could have performed. In the fullness of time, new life burst forth and Rachel was first to give praise.

H. C. Leupold states, "Quite humbly Rachel, who early in her marriage may have been a more or less haughty and self-sufficient personage, now gives God the glory and rejoices that He has taken away her reproach. Sterility brought reproach as though

God had deemed a wife unworthy of children. Rachel still stands on the lower level of faith when she makes this remark, for she thinks only of the sovereign power of God. Yet her experience of divine help raises her faith to the higher level when she asks for grace from the faithful covenant God Yahweh."[5]

Rachel's testimony recorded in Genesis 30:22-24 was:

God in His time hearkened to my voice;
God in His mercy has taken away my reproach;
God has added to my life what was indeed impossible;
God has used my barrenness as a lesson in brokenness.

The lesson of jealousy and sovereignty brought about increased faithfulness, a greater love and dependence upon God, a purified heart, an overflowing sense of joy, a deep-seated peace, long-suffering, and a renewed sense of worship. Rachel reaped not only the fruit of the womb but also the fruit of the Spirit.

If God is allowing barrenness in your life today, it is only to deepen the level of your fruitfulness for tomorrow.

Lessons from the School of Barrenness

In this chapter we have discovered that:

- Envy is accompanied by some degree of hatred or malignity and desires the depreciation of another human being.
- Envy can be traced to areas where we compare ourselves with others.
- God will not allow human ambitions or human services to produce the offspring of His promises.
- The lessons of patience, faith and submission are taught in the classroom of barrenness.
- Whatever spirit dominates the leader will infiltrate the ministry.

- God-kind of jealousy is a zeal of love and of right perspective, not a self-love.
- Leaders position the ministry; God provides and produces the offspring.

(((Making It Personal)))

1. Has the Holy Spirit used this chapter to spotlight areas where you have fallen into the comparison trap of envy?
2. In what areas of your church, ministry or personal life are you striving to fulfill a promise that only God can birth?
3. What are some of the attitudes that most concern you about your congregation, staff or even family that you know have filtered down through your own undealt-with stuff? Do you want to be changed?
4. Have you been feeding on others' failures or weaknesses? Do you really want to see your neighbor's ministry grow, even beyond your own? If not, will you say yes to a season of barrenness so God can bring forth a greater harvest in you later?

Notes

1. *Webster's New Twentieth Century Dictionary—2nd Edition*, (U.S.A.: Collins World Publishers, 1978).
2. Jack Hayford, *Pastors of Promise* (Ventura, Calif.: Regal, 1997), p. 161.
3. Ralph G. Turnbull, *Minister's Obstacles* (Grand Rapids: Baker Books, 1972—originally published by Fleming H. Revel, 1946), p. 37.
4. Ibid., p. 34.
5. H. C. Leupold, *Exposition of Genesis—Vol. II* (Grand Rapids: Baker Books, 1987), p. 815.

9

Manoah's Wife: Lessons in Ownership

‎◡

He who finds his life will lose it, and he who loses

his life for My sake will find it.

—*Matthew 10:39*

As I crumbled the Styrofoam cup in my hand I said out loud, "Thank you, cup, for your willingness to be used. Now, to your destiny...crunch, into the garbage can." The destiny of that cup had been determined by its purpose, and I had desired the coffee, not the Styrofoam cup. The cup had served its purpose as a coffee-carrying vessel, and I wasn't praying or asking for any kind of a *rhema* word about Styrofoam cups when God spoke, not audibly, but by a sure Holy Spirit impression upon my inner man, a clear inner voice.

A Scripture verse came to mind, "But we have this treasure in earthen vessels, that the excellence of the power may be of God and not of us" (2 Cor. 4:7).

I paused, locking my mind for a few moments as I considered this quickened verse, *We have treasure in earthen vessels.* God then simply impressed a word upon me in a flash, a direct hit, right to the hidden parts of my heart: *Ownership. You must give up ownership.* My heart immediately responded, knowing God was using my innocent cup experience to reveal something in my life. My response was, "Father God, thank You for bringing this to my attention and for removing this from my life. Thank you."

That was the end of my divine encounter...but only the beginning of the journey to fulfill my prayer. I had naively believed a simple prayer would deliver me from this not-so-simple problem: ownership. I didn't fully understand what God was after. I had always given God my best, given Him praise for our successes. I had not tried to own anything in our ministry or church. Throughout the next several years all this would change: our ministry, our church, our future and our rights to certain things.

Lord, Is That Really You?

I was in my car on my way to deliver a decision I had made about my future. The decision was monumental in the direction our ministries would take. The presence of God invaded my car. It was definitely real and I wasn't expecting it. The Lord's voice to me in that instant was staggering, *Lay your vision down and serve another's.*

Some might stumble at my use of the Lord's voice at a very precarious time in my life and ministry. Should a leader put that much stock in a spiritual experience, a spiritual "heavy" of an inner voice? Jack Hayford offers the following encouragement about hearing the voice of God:

Notwithstanding that the Bible overflows with case studies of God's speaking to people personally, by name, giving insight, instruction and direction at specific points in their lives and leadership duties, a devastating twist on truth has taken place. In far too many quarters, accepted orthodoxy only believes those recorded encounters "happened," but it is considered unorthodox, indeed presumptuous, to think they do happen.[1]

I'm not really given to subjective experiences such as voices, dreams and impressions. I believe the Holy Spirit can and does speak to people and that God speaks to me. But encounters of this magnitude have only occurred a few times in my Christian life. This was a "life directional" word. Our vision had been set. How could I lay it down? It was a great vision, and God had given me the inspiration. Why should I lay it down? We had mapped out our state with a church-planting strategy. Sixty-seven places would be targeted and we were on our way to fulfilling the vision. Now came a word to stop—and even more astonishing— to serve someone else's vision.

This was my first encounter with God's secret ways and means committee to remove my tight grip on my vision, my ministry and my future. Ownership was now becoming an issue I could identify, but still not connect to my simple prayer, "God, thank You for bringing this to my attention and for removing it from my life." God had my attention now and God had His intention: remove ownership from my spirit.

I obeyed the Lord that day, first in my car at the side of the road weeping, praying, having a spiritual visitation. I had no human idea of what that day in my car meant, no idea that my giving up ownership of our church vision would actually seal my destiny to a future that only God could put together.

The Most Difficult Sunday of Our Church Journey

As I stood before our congregation, our beloved church that we had planted, nurtured and loved with everything we had, I prepared to announce the news. We were resigning as pastors and moving back to Portland to succeed the pastor of our mother church. I had on several occasions stated my lifetime commitment, and now we were leaving. It was the most difficult and emotional decision of my adult life. I was, we were, giving up our success, the fruit of our labor and our identity. We owned this vision. Our fingerprints were everywhere, our own unique markings.

My Styrofoam cup encounter was now making sense to me, and I didn't like it. Yes, I did pray that simple "do whatever it takes, go ahead, root out the ownership attitude in my life" prayer. But this was more than I bargained for! The church had

○

Barrenness is God's method for exposing and removing our grip, our tightfisted attitude of ownership, in order to move us into a new realm of ministry.

○

not been my product, but God's. The church we planted had grown by God's grace, God-empowered preaching, teaching, counseling and vision casting. This church had been God's child, a God seed, a God giving of life. I thought I knew that! The words of 1 Corinthians 3:5-7 echoed in my mind:

Who then is Paul, and who is Apollos, but ministers through whom you believed, as the Lord gave to each one? I planted, Apollos watered, but God gave the increase. So then neither he who plants is anything, nor he who waters, but God who gives the increase.

Removing Our Grip

When no human possibility exists for growth or success, we usually turn to God easily, giving Him all ownership of our ministries and churches. But when leaders are able to produce through their unique giftings, abilities, personalities, methods and creativity, there is a certain sense of *It's mine. I gave my life and I deserve recognition, reward and respect. I bought it, paid for it, and I own it.*

Barrenness is God's method for exposing and removing our grip, our tightfisted attitude of ownership in order to move us into a new realm of ministry. The school of barrenness allows us to exhaust ourselves, come to the end of fleshly carnal ambitions and move us into the supernatural realm. After all, "we have this treasure in earthen vessels, that the excellence of the power may be of God and not of us." We are dependent upon God's grace for new life in our ministries and churches.

The New English Bible translates 2 Corinthians 4:7 this way: "We are no better than pots of earthenware to contain this treasure, and this proves that such transcendent power does not come from us, but is God's alone."

"Which would you rather be? A vessel of your own design, based upon your finite mind and limited creativity, power and wisdom—a vessel of limited use and passing value? Or a vessel of His design, based upon His infinite wisdom, love and power—a vessel of unlimited use and eternal, unsearchable value?"[2]

Vessels of Purpose:
The Barren Women of Scripture

Three barren women in Scripture well illustrate the point of giving up ownership—all were vessels containing a treasure. The treasure, in each case, was highly esteemed; the vessel was quickly forgotten. These barren women were brought to a place where they could, with conviction, say, "If you break the bands of my barrenness, I will give you the child. You name him. You use him. You take ownership of him." It was the pain, suffering and dying to self that caused Manoah's wife to give up Samson, Hannah to give up Samuel and Elizabeth to give up John the Baptist. Barrenness aids us in realizing our source of success and allows God's blessings, miracles and purposes to flow through us. A dead person doesn't have much of a grip!

These three women graduated from the school of barrenness,

humbly and graciously changed by learning to relinquish ownership of God's ministries, blessings and miracle provision. Their
sons would not belong to them; they would only be the vessels
to carry the purposes of God.

Manoah's Wife	Samson	Deliverer
Hannah	Samuel	Prophet and Judge
Elizabeth	John the Baptist	Prophet and Forerunner to Christ

All three barren women are beautiful examples of how the
most unpleasant and untoward circumstances can produce character that blesses the world. The Bible has been called the "World's
Gallery of Lasting Fame," and in this gallery, the barren women of
Scripture have their place. Manoah's wife, Hannah and Elizabeth all
produced world-class leaders who stood in times of spiritual and
historical transition. They stood at the intersections of history
where the circumstances merited a bona fide miracle through the
messenger of God. Each one paid a high price to offer up to the
world a deliverer, a prophet-judge and a prophet-forerunner.

The leadership roles of Samson, Samuel and John the Baptist
were all made possible by these unique, godly women who
would endure the test of delay, patiently praying, painfully living.
Ridicule, criticism, accusation—the cruel and scurrilous tongues
were always present. These women suffered, unknowingly, for
the purposes of God to be fulfilled at the divine moment. The test
was pressed upon them and they grew strong in spirit; they
matured in character.

Manoah's wife, Hannah and Elizabeth were the vessels who
would carry and nurture these miracle children to the place of
awesome ministry. They deserve our respect and appreciation—
so do the many God-shaped ministries that have spent most of
their time in the wilderness of barrenness, waiting for God to
release His divine purposes through their lives. They are well
hidden under the shadow of God's dealing, placed carefully like
an arrow in God's quiver, waiting to be shot forth.

Manoah's Barren Wife: The Mother of Samson

The setting and background are found in Judges 13—16...the short glimpse of Samson's mother and then the life of Samson. Jephthah, another leader raised up by God, was delivering the tribes on the east of the Jordan from the oppression of the Ammonites. The Philistine oppression on the west side of Jordan had gone on for 40 years. The Philistines had plundered Israel in the closing years of backslidden high priest Eli. The Philistines had taken the Ark of the Covenant but were sorely judged by God and quickly returned the Ark to the Israelites. God was raising up a new deliverer. His name would be called Samson. Samson would appear in the fullness of time with a supernatural strength to deliver Israel from the Philistines. Samson was a miracle child, his mother a barren woman whose hope was in the mercy of God.

Barrenness: A Test in God's Timing

God would break the bands when his purposes would best be implemented. Manoah and his wife had no way to properly comprehend the enormous task their son would be called to. He would be nationally famous. Throughout the history of humanity their son would be known and remembered as the man who had secret supernatural strength. How could they grasp the magnitude of their barrenness?

Manoah's wife appeared to be just another unfortunate woman in Israel—just another childless mother. This couple probably didn't sit around discussing the sovereign delays of God through their barrenness. The purpose of God that would be released through Samson's birth and the history-making events he would determine were not part of their dinnertime discussions.

"Manoah, how is your wife? Any change in this curse, this affliction?" was a normal question posed to them. While her husband's name is preserved, she herself remains nameless although the Talmud says she bore the name of Hazelelponi or Zelelponi and that she was of the tribe of Judah.[3] Zelelponi means "the shadow fell on me," and Manoah's wife was certainly one who dwelt under the shadow of the Almighty in becoming mother to the strongest man who ever lived. She also dwelt under the shadow of barrenness, a shadow that would be eclipsed by a joyful breakthrough in God's time.

Manoah's wife would receive a gift, a miracle that would change the destiny of all Israel. They were not cursed, unfortunate, forgotten. Poor Manoah and his wife. What a shame! No. They were in the season of preparation to bring forth the deliverer, the voice and power of God into a generation. They would receive an angelic visitation, a sure word of direction and the opportunity to usher in the era of freedom all Israel dreamed about.

God's gifts to us are usually regulated in their extent by our capacity for receiving them. Manoah's wife had a receptive heart and believed the promises of God to her. Her prayers were in time answered and the bands of barrenness broken. She understood God's overruling throughout her barren years and rejoiced in the gift of leadership granted through her son, Samson.

Barrenness Broken: The Samson Dilemma

Manoah's wife had successfully graduated from the school of barrenness. She bore a son. Samson's name (Hebrew: *Shimshown*) was tied to the strength and power of God, his name meaning "the strength of the sun" (Hebrew: *Shemesh*; see Ps. 19:5,6; 84:11).[4] He was to rule Israel as a delivering judge for 20 years, but not without compromise, sinful behavior and blatant disobedience to God's laws and ways.

Samson's sinful patterns and weakness for seductive women caused great sorrow and deep disappointment to his mother. She had prayed for this savior of Israel for years and now her answered prayer failed to produce the result she had hoped for. She could not control Samson's power. His power had been given by God, yet could be used for his own pleasures. This was confusing and disappointing, not only to Samson's parents but also to Israel.

The bands of barrenness may be removed from our ministries

or churches by a divine act of God's favor and grace. God may grant success in every area as His favor causes prosperity in every realm. What we don't know is what success will do once it has been birthed. What will power do once it has been given life? Samson represents anointing unleashed, power released and manifestation of the awesome strength of God revealed.

All ministries and churches welcome a visitation of God's miraculous power. Some are desperate for God to show up. The cry for more power, more miracles, a more awesome working of God can be heard around the world. My question is, What happens when Samson is birthed, honored and released? Can we handle the authority and power of God, or will it pervert us, change us and ultimately destroy us?

Samson, a New Anointing, a New Power, a New Test

Samson killed a lion, 30 Philistines and 1,000 men, to mention just a few of his awesome acts. The strongest bands wrapped around him, he broke with ease. He carried off the gates of Gaza and destroyed the temple of Dagon. He moved into an unparalleled realm of spiritual power and authority—one which the church desires today. But his newfound power did not motivate him to conquer his blatant, sinful, sexual relations with foreign women. The deadly results of Samson's self-indulgence after breaking his Nazirite vow appear in their dark and ominous order in Judges 16:

Self-confidence	"I will go out" (v. 20);
Self-ignorance	"He knew not" (v. 20);
Self-weakness	"The Philistines laid hold on him" (v. 21);
Self-darkness	"They put out his eyes" (v. 21);
Self-degradation	"They brought him down to Gaza" (vv. 1-3);
Self-bondage	"They bound him with fetters" (v. 21);
Self-drudgery	"He did grind in the prison house" (v. 21);
Self-humiliation	"Call for Samson that we may make sport of him" (vv. 25,27).[5]

Every heart, whether regenerate or unregenerate, craves power in one form or another. J. Oswald Sanders says, "...not a power under our control. God does not give us a something—power—which we can control and use as we will. Simon coveted the power which he saw Peter exercise and asked, 'Give me also this power...' But Peter said to him, 'Your silver perish with you because you thought you could obtain the gift of God with money.'"[6]

As God breaks bands of barrenness, we move into fruitfulness and into another level of temptation and testing. As God provides the grace of enlargement, influence and success, we are tempted with ownership attitudes. As God loans us His power, we are tempted to use the power for our own purposes and allow mixture, compromise and blatant disobedience to go unchecked. We must keep our hunger focused on *the God of power* rather than *the power of God*.

As the blankets of barrenness are pulled back, prepare to face your Samson tests. How you respond will leave an eternal imprint on your world, your generation and the population of His kingdom.

Lessons from the School of Barrenness

In this chapter we have discovered that:

- When leaders are able to produce through their unique giftings, abilities, personalities, methods and creativity, *ownership* is the result.
- Barrenness is God's method for exposing and removing our grip, our tightfisted attitude of ownership in order to move us into a new realm of ministry.
- Only when we can die to the vision, do we have the assurance that God owns it. A dead person doesn't have much of a grip!
- God's gifts to us are usually regulated in their extent by our capacity for receiving them.
- Success is a test. What we don't know is what success

will do once it has been birthed. What will power do once it has been given life?

- We must focus on God, not the power He can give us.
- God loans us His power, but we are tempted to use the power for our own purposes and allow compromise and blatant disobedience to go unchecked.
- When the power lines get crossed, the Church gets hurt.

((Making It Personal))

1. Has God given you a vision that you have sweated and toiled for? Will you lay it down to serve another?
2. Have you died to your will and risen to God's? Where do you need to loosen your grip?
3. Are there still areas in your life where your power struggle with the world could cause you to fall into Satan's trap? Ask God to show you.
4. What is your real motive for seeing God's power released in your church, in your ministry, in your life?

Notes

1. Jack Hayford, *Pastors of Promise* (Ventura, Calif.: Regal), p. 170.
2. Charles Stanley, *The Blessings of Brokenness* (Grand Rapids: Zondervan), p. 13.
3. Herbert Lockyer, *All the Women of the Bible* (Grand Rapids: Zondervan), p. 185.
4. G. W. Bromiley, Editor, *International Standard Bible Encyclopedia Vol. 4*, (Grand Rapids, William B. Eerdman, 1982), p. 309.
5. Herbert Lockyer, *All the Men of the Bible* (Grand Rapids: Zondervan), page 292.
6. J. Oswald Sanders, *Spiritual Lessons* (Chicago: Moody Press), p. 55.

10

Hannah: Lessons in Overcoming Satanic Attacks

ʊ

For we do not wrestle against flesh and blood, but
against principalities, against powers, against the
rulers of the darkness of this age, against spiritual
hosts of wickedness in the heavenly places.

—*Ephesians 6:12*

The story of Hannah, the mother of Samuel the great prophet-judge, is one that touches the emotions as few other stories in Scripture. Hannah's story is found in 1 Samuel 1:1—2:21, and takes place during one of Israel's key historical turning points. Samuel the prophet-judge would lead Israel out of the turbulent times of the judges into the prosperous times of the kings. Samuel the prophet would be a king-maker, a king-anointer and a king-confronter. His mother, Hannah, would be the foundation for his long and influential ministry to Israel. Again, God, by His sovereign hand, prepared the way for greatness through a barren woman's life of pain, sorrow, rejection and humiliation.

Hannah's husband Elkanah was a man of Ramathaim Zophim, the mountains of Ephraim, or Ramah, the shortened name for Ramathaim Zophim, where Samuel was born, lived, labored and was buried. Elkanah had two wives, Peninnah and Hannah. Peninnah had children; Hannah was barren. Elkanah was a direct descendant of Zuph, whose family line is recorded in 1 Chronicles 6:26,27,31,32. This family line identifies Samuel as a member of the Kohathite branch of the tribe of Levi and a descendant of Tabernacle and Temple musicians (see 1 Chron. 6:16,22,31-38).[1]

Hannah: Grace in the Face of Disgrace

Hannah's barren experiences offer insights into ministries and churches that are experiencing spiritual barrenness. The name Hannah means "grace, graciousness or favor."[2] And as her name suggests, barrenness had not worked a disgruntled, murmuring, cynical attitude in this woman of character.

Barrenness in ancient times was the ultimate tragedy for a married woman because her husband's hopes and dreams were dependent upon her providing him with a male heir to perpetuate his name and to inherit his estate. Hannah not only bore her own sorrow, but also the constant sorrow of being unable to fulfill her husband's dreams. Add to this the constant harassment of Peninnah, Elkanah's fruitful wife, and Hannah's own personal humiliation, and you have a combination for deep brokenness.

Every year Elkanah went up to Shiloh, about a 16-mile journey, to sacrifice and celebrate God's blessing upon their home (see 1 Sam. 1:3). These festival celebrations were times of rejoicing in God's abundant provisions, blessings and goodness. But not for Hannah! This annual trip was the deepest and darkest hour of her year. To say she dreaded or hated this trek would be a gross understatement.

It was the time of year Elkanah would praise Peninnah for the sons and daughters she had given him, blessing each child by name. There in the shadows, standing alone, heartbroken and humiliated, would be Hannah. Elkanah loved Hannah deeply. He would attempt to offer some healing to her wounds by giving her a "double portion" (v. 5) of the sacrifice meat or the harvest offering. But she was barren. No future. No hope. No children to bless. No celebration over her offspring.

Perhaps it was Hannah's barrenness that had prompted Elkanah to take Peninnah as his second wife, which only added to the deep void in Hannah's heart. Peninnah, Hannah's provoker, directly attacked her unchanging barrenness. However, the sorrow, humiliation and attacks only worked in Hannah a deeper grace and graciousness that would be foundational to the awesome ministry of Samuel, the great and wise prophet-judge.

Shame at Shiloh

I'm sure every church and ministry in a barren season can identify with Hannah. Going up to your Shiloh is like attending your particular denomination or movement's annual pastors' conference. It's a time of celebration, rejoicing, testimonies of God's goodness and divine provision. Pastors and church leaders talk openly of church expansion, new building programs, new evangelistic outreaches, new membership ideas. Pastors speak of the pressure of adding multiple services, and you're thinking of your one sparsely attended service. You stand in the shadows hoping the conversation doesn't turn your way: "How's your Sunday attendance? How many new converts have you had this year? What new building programs are you launching?"

Your heart is filled with sorrow and guilt as you question your calling, maybe even your own relationship with God. It is a festival for most, but a funeral for you. Death is creeping into your vision and your faith dwindles as you compare your barren year with the fruitfulness of others.

Shiloh Rivalry

Then it happens. The enemy seizes an opportunity, an open window into your soul that is vulnerable to his hellish assault. "Now," he says, "now is the time to shoot my arrows of discouragement, depression and accusation."

First Samuel 1:6 reads, "And her rival also provoked her severely, to make her miserable, because the Lord had closed her womb." Peninnah is used by the enemy to attack Hannah in a weak moment. This is a picture of what our enemy, the devil, will do to every Hannah ministry or church. Peninnah, the fellow wife, would vex Hannah bitterly over her misfortune. She would annoy her, taunt her and provoke her mercilessly.

The Hebrew word for "rival" (*tsarah*) comes from the verb *tsarar* which means to show hostility toward. The noun form is also translated as "adversary or enemy" (see Lev. 18:18).[3] We have a rival. It's not other ministries or churches, but the evil kingdom of darkness with all its demonic hosts that are out to destroy our souls. As we see in Luke 4:13, the barren Hannah ministries and churches will encounter this enemy continually, seasonally, at opportune times: "Now when the devil had ended every temptation, he departed from him until an opportune time." The enemy seeks those moments of opportunity, usually when we least expect his arrival. His timing is calculated, strategized, studied and directed toward these opportune moments (see 2 Cor. 4:4; Eph. 2:2; 6:10-17; John 12:31; 1 John 5:19). Opportune times for satanic attack occur:

- When we are experiencing seasons of fruitfulness (see Gen. 49:22-26);
- When we take steps to sacrificially serve or give (see Gen. 15:11);
- When we have a genuine spiritual breakthrough (see Exod. 14:15,16);
- When we are offering up serious prayer intercession (see Dan. 9:3,4; 10:12-14);

- When we are leading, but in need of cleansing (see Zech. 3:1-6).

Peninnah "thundered against" Hannah, provoking Hannah with evil words, words intended to cause the most embarrassment and the deepest shame. Hannah's adversary provoked her, constantly irritating her. First Samuel 1:6 uses a forceful sentence structure and a forceful double use of the word "provoke" (Hebrew: *ka'as*) to emphasize the depth and constancy of this harassment.[4] The word "provoke" has the idea of "excite, put into inward commotion, confuse or torment."[5] This is exactly what the enemy will do if we allow him to during these seasons of barrenness.

Shiloh, Satan's Stomping Ground

First Samuel 1:7 says, "Year by year, when she went up to the house of the Lord, that she provoked her, therefore she wept and did not eat." Attacks on Hannah came around visits to the house of the Lord, a unique timing of the enemy. Satan provokes us at the time when we should be enjoying God's presence, celebrating God's victories and ministering to others in the house of the Lord. The attack is on our ground, our place of prayer and worship, our church, our ministry times.

Hannah's rival took special delight in using the annual pilgrimage to Shiloh as an occasion for continued provocation, badgering Hannah to the point of tears. Just as Elkanah showed his love to Hannah at every sacrificial festival, so did Peninnah repeat her provocation.

Be aware of your enemy's desire to attack when you visit your Shiloh. Shiloh represents several pertinent truths to every leader who is seeking to fulfill God's dream and vision.

Shiloh Is...

Shiloh is the center around which activities involving a vision and the appropriating of that vision take place (see Josh. 18:1,8-10; 19:51; 21:2).

Shiloh is the place where God's people gather and give God the praise and glory for keeping every promise He has made to His people. The word, prophecy, encouragement and discernment are spoken here (see Josh. 21:45; 22:9).

Shiloh is the place where Satan is foiled in his attempts to twist the vision for his own purposes, and his strongholds on God's people are broken. There is a special anointing here for discerning God's truth (see Josh. 22:10-34).

Shiloh is a place of comfort and peace for God's people. It is a place of peace and hope when despair exists elsewhere (see 1 Sam. 1:9,11).

Shiloh is a place to meet God and obtain the unobtainable desires of the heart (see 1 Sam. 1:17).

Shiloh is a place of sacrifice and returning to God the gift He has placed in our hands (see 1 Sam. 1:24).

Shiloh is a place where barrenness (spiritual, emotional and physical) is turned to victory and fruitfulness in God (see 1 Sam. 2:1-10).

Shiloh is a place where a dedicated prophet of God can grow and mature in the ways of the Lord (see 1 Sam. 2:11,18,21,26).

Shiloh is a place of vision in a world that cannot see, a place of plenty in the midst of famine (see 1 Sam. 3:1-18).

Shiloh is a place where prophets are confirmed as prophets (see 1 Sam. 3:19,20).

Shiloh is a place where the Lord appears and is revealed to His prophets by a Living Word (see 1 Sam. 3:21).

Shiloh is a place from which the word of the Lord goes forth to all the nations (see 1 Sam. 4:1).[6]

Let your heart be strengthened as you absorb these words: *Your God will always pour in more grace, more promises, more healing, more strength as the enemy seeks to destroy you.*

Maybe these descriptions of Hannah from the first chapter of 1 Samuel are yours:

Barren, no children (v. 2);
The Lord closed her womb (v. 5);
And her rival (v. 6);
Provoked her severely (v. 6);
Made her miserable (v. 6);
She wept and did not eat (v. 7);
Heart grieved (v. 8);
Bitterness of soul (v. 10);
Wept in anguish (v. 10);
Sorrowful spirit (v. 15);
Complaint and grief (v. 16).

Breaking Barrenness Through Intercession

If you find yourself identifying with Hannah's sorrow, emotional turmoil and attack of the enemy, then you must identify with Hannah's turning to the Lord through intercessory prayer.

☻

Barrenness is an opportunity for the devil to attack, but it is also an opportunity to take your brokenness, sorrow and grief to God with strong, prayerful intercession.

☻

Barrenness is an opportunity for the devil to attack, but it is also an opportunity to take your brokenness, sorrow and grief to God with strong, prayerful intercession. First Samuel 1:10 says, "she was in bitterness of soul," but she didn't allow bitter experiences to mark her soul. She journeyed past the bitter taste of barrenness to a place of deep intercessory prayer. Hannah's prayer in her barren state could be a model prayer for every barren ministry or church. The prayer is recorded in 1 Samuel 1:11-19.

The Vow
Then she made a "vow" (v. 11)
A vow may be either to perform (see Gen. 28:20) or to abstain from (see Ps. 82:2) an act in return for God's favor (see Num. 21:1-8). It is no sin to vow or not to vow, but if a vow is made, it is as sacredly binding as an oath (see Deut. 23:21-23). What is already the Lord's, such as the first of the harvest and firstborn of the flock, might be redeemed (see Lev. 23; Num. 3:44,45). It was proper for Hannah to give Samuel to the Lord as a Nazirite.[7] Hannah's vow was a reflection of the depth of her desire and her brokenness. How moving, this pouring out of prayer by Hannah before God in His house, vowing that she would give up ownership completely and give back this son exclusively for God's use:

> O Lord of hosts, if You will indeed look on the affliction of Your maidservant and remember me, and not forget Your maidservant, but will give Your maidservant a male child, then I will give him to the Lord all the days of his life, and no razor shall come upon his head (1 Sam. 1:11).

The Heart Prayer
"Hannah spoke in her heart; only her lips moved" (v. 13)
Hannah's prayer was hidden within the secret compartment of her soul. This would be a prayer birthed out of her distress. Her heart was filled with the words of her rival and hurts of her journey. It would be from this altar she would find the words to pray. These words had been born in sorrow, birthed in her tears and meditated on for years. She prayed "in the presence of God." She literally entered into and enjoyed the manifest presence of God during her intercessory prayer times. She had learned that the only place of comfort, encouragement and renewal was in the presence of Jehovah. This was her hiding place, her place of intimacy, her place of familiar ground. In His presence is where she would find the grace to make a vow, the grace to pour out her heart and never speak out loud. Her prayer was silent because it was deep inside her, mixed with a felt presence of God. She

prayed "in her heart" to herself, silently, sacredly, a divine work hidden from the eyes of Eli the high priest.

The Pouring Out of Petitionary Prayer
"Have poured out my soul before the Lord" (v. 15).

This is a vivid idiom for praying earnestly and passionately before the Lord (see Ps. 42:4; 62:8; Lam. 2:19). Hannah was not intoxicated with strong drink, but was intoxicated with a strong manifest presence of God. She was under a deep "burden" of prayer. She was deeply troubled and "burdened in spirit"; thus she poured out her soul unto God. Hannah's prayer consisted of great sighing, grief and brokenness all put into words that only her heart could speak. The mouth could not articulate the depth of her petition. She was barren and childless, but she was not prayerless! Her pain found a refuge in prayer, in a specific kind of praying. It was in this manifest presence of God that the bonds of barrenness burst open. Her tragedy would turn to triumph, for prayer had won the victory. No one else could see, but at that moment Hannah was conceiving Samuel in the privacy of her prayer with God. She had learned that prayer is powerful, even when unuttered or unexpressed, sending the secrets of the soul directly to the throne of God.

Petition Granted
"Then Eli answered and said, 'Go in peace, and the God of Israel grant your petition which you have asked of Him'" (v. 17).

Hannah would receive the honor and favor of God requested in her petition. She would no longer be the barren, harassed woman, sorrowful and grieved. She would now be blessed with favor and honor from God. Her intercession would be gloriously fulfilled. From the moment her intercession was finished, her countenance was changed and she was no longer sorrowful but joyful. She could eat and return to living a happy, fulfilled life:

> And [Hannah] said, "Let your maidservant find favor in your sight." So the woman went her way and ate, and her face was no longer sad (v. 18).

The Vow Fulfilled

"As long as he lives he shall be lent to the Lord" (v. 28).

Hannah's barrenness was broken and God gave her Samuel, the great prophet-judge of Israel. Hannah fulfilled her vow exactly as she had made it. She took Samuel when he was weaned and presented him to Eli at the Temple (see 1 Sam. 1:24-28). Hannah then sang her song of thanksgiving, a bursting forth of her grateful heart, a song filled with exaltation to the Lord. The spiritual lyrics of Hannah are equal to any of the Psalms and eloquent with the divine attributes of power, holiness, knowledge, majesty and grace.[8]

May every barren ministry and church sing the song of Hannah as a faith declaration to God's intentions for our future.

Hannah's Song
1 Samuel 2:1-10

My heart rejoices in the Lord; my horn is exalted in the Lord. I smile at my enemies, because I rejoice in Your salvation. No one is holy like the Lord, for there is none besides You, nor is there any rock like our God. Talk no more so very proudly; let no arrogance come from your mouth, for the Lord is the God of knowledge; and by Him actions are weighed. The bows of the mighty men are broken, and those who stumbled are girded with strength. Those who were full have hired themselves out for bread, and the hungry have ceased to hunger. Even the barren has borne seven, and she who has many children has become feeble. The Lord kills and makes alive; He brings down to the grave and brings up. The Lord makes poor and makes rich; He brings low and lifts up. He raises the poor from the dust and lifts the beggar from the ash heap, to set them among princes and make them inherit the throne of glory. For the pillars of the earth are the Lord's, and He has set the world upon them. He will guard the feet of His saints, but the wicked shall be silent in darkness. For by strength no man shall prevail. The adversaries of the Lord shall be broken in pieces; from heaven He will thunder against them. The Lord will judge the ends of the earth. He will give strength to His king, and exalt the horn of His anointed.

Lessons from the School of Barrenness

In this chapter we have discovered that:

- Barrenness exposes the heart. As in Hannah's case, we can remain free from a disgruntled, murmuring, cynical attitude by leaning on God.
- The temptation to resent others can be overcome with the knowledge that the enemy (the powers of hell and darkness) is the enemy, not other people, places or ministries.
- Beware: Your greatest moments of opportunity become the opportune times for Satan's greatest attacks.
- Our rival, the devil, provokes us at the time when we should be enjoying God's presence, celebrating God's victories and ministering to others in the house of the Lord.
- The more the enemy seeks to destroy you, the greater the outpouring of God's grace in your life. God's power to rebuild is always greater than Satan's power to destroy.
- Those walking in barrenness will find refuge, not in casual inquiries of God, but in deep, heartfelt intercessory prayer.

((Making It Personal))

1. In what ways is your rival, the kingdom of hell and darkness, attempting to provoke you to bitterness? Is it self-pity? Is it jealousy? Is it unforgiveness?
2. Reflect on the circumstances just prior to your season of

barrenness. Were you on the crest of an opportunity? If so, what vulnerabilities gave Satan a window through which to attack?

3. How has the enemy sought to steal the joy of your Shiloh? Will you make the choice to enter into a season of praise?

4. What part does intercessory prayer play in your life? Are you a casual inquirer or a promise-keeping, promise-seeking worshiper who is willing to give your heart's desire back to God?

Notes

1. Frank Gabelein, *Expositor's Bible Commentary* (Grand Rapids: Zondervan, 1995), Vol. 3, p. 590.
2. G. W. Bromiley, Editor, *International Standard Bible Encyclopedia Vol. 2*, (Grand Rapids, William B. Eerdman, 1982), p. 613.
3. *BDB*, p. 865; *TWOT*, #1974b.
4. *BDB*, pp. 494-495; *TWOT* #1016.
5. Noah Webster, *America's Dictionary of the English Language* (San Francisco: Foundation for American Christian Education, 1928).
6. Carl Townsend, *Strategic Visions for the Evangelization of Portland* (Portland, Oreg., March 31, 1995).
7. William Eerdman, *The New Bible Dictionary* (Downer's Grove, Ill.: Intervarsity Press, 1982), p. 1313.
8. Herbert Lockyer, *All the Women of the Bible* (Grand Rapids: Zondervan, 1967), p. 66.

11

Elizabeth: Lessons in God's Timing

○

The steps of a good man are ordered by the Lord,

and He delights in his way....I have been young,

and now am old; Yet I have not seen

the righteous forsaken.

—*Psalm 37:23,25*

The trip to Fuller Seminary was more than a geographical change for me. As a nondenominational, charismatic pastor, it was an emotional-theological change. I was leaving familiar ground to venture into doctoral-level studies in a seminary. This was highly unusual for the movement of pastors and churches with which I had been affiliated. We believed the local church was the ground for training, and the Bible itself was sufficient for aiding pastors in building great churches. We of course read other books, and our mother church had established a Bible college, but courses on church growth were not offered. We believed God was responsible for growing the church, not human-made ideas compromising the pattern in His Word.

Here I was walking on the campus of Fuller Seminary, seeking to enroll in the doctoral studies in the School of World Missions and the Institute of Church Growth. I was nervous to say the least, doubtful, yet filled with a sense of expectation. I wanted to learn how to grow churches. I didn't want to lack any theological foundations, relevant methodologies or new innovative ideas. Church growth training here I come!

This was my first encounter with Dr. C. Peter Wagner. I had read his books, but never personally met him, and yet he went out of his way to accompany me in making the rounds to enroll. My first class on church growth was "Your Church and Church Growth," exactly what I desired. The course description read, "This course is designed to make you a more effective Christian leader. As you systematically work through the contents you will find yourself developing 'church growth eyes.' You will be challenged by new and exciting opportunities for the future."

Church Growth U, Here I Am

I became a serious student of church growth, taking classes and reading more than a hundred books on church growth from every angle and diverse background. I read, wrote papers, talked with church-growth professors and pastors of large, growing churches. The learning process was life changing and ministry changing. I would have the knowledge to change a church from any nongrowth level into a growing church. Church growth philosophy is based on the scriptural assumption that the church is designed to grow, and all other nongrowth ideas are unscriptural excuses.

Those against church growth were very opposed to the dominant thought perceived in church growth: *I can grow my church.* Robert K. Hudnut's *Church Growth Is Not the Point* states the other side. Its protest is directed against all ideas of churchly success as a guarantee of Christian effectiveness. That means the point of the church's existence is whether the church is true to the gospel, not whether it grows numerically. Hadnut has the following to say:

One final slogan that contains a lot of unexamined and questionable assumptions is church growth. Its philosophy undergirds a great deal of thinking and planning to do with the church's mission in the world. Perhaps your church is committing itself to an outreach program and you see this as a heavenly mandate to increase and multiply. But let's be clear that witness and numerical growth are not the same. As I read the New Testament, the Lord's commission to His church is to be faithful in witness, not necessarily successful in growing. You could say that whenever growing is spoken of in the New Testament church, the implied subject of the sentence is God, as in 1 Corinthians 3:7. It is God's church we are talking about and He alone can produce the growth. "I will build my church," Matthew 16:18, runs counter to a lot of popular sentiment current today, expressed by those who imagine that they can bring in the kingdom of God with a slide rule and a set of log tables.[1]

In the arguments for and against church growth, both sides have biblical insights. The proper combination for healthy church growth is the power of God and the responsibility of man. The key, of course, is to use both, with balance and wisdom, to bring about desired growth. The frustration is when a pastor who has a non-growing church, a barren church, puts into practice all the points from church-growth literature and does not see results. This is when knowledge of principles and patterns falls hurtfully short and the mystery of church growth is encountered. "I have done everything I was supposed to do. I followed the plan carefully and there are no apparent results." This dilemma is what I have come to describe as "The Elizabeth Factor."

When You're Doing Everything You Know

Zacharias and Elizabeth were doing all the rights things in the right way with a righteous motive. They were model examples of following the pattern God had laid down, yet, they were without child—barren:

> And they were both righteous before God, walking in all the commandments and ordinances of the Lord blameless. But they had no child, because Elizabeth was barren, and they were both well advanced in years (Luke 1:6,7).

Elizabeth's childlessness was not caused by a lack of righteousness or obedience before or unto God. "Righteous before God" means that when they were standing before God's judgment bar, they received His sentence of approval.[2] But to be childless brought sorrow and often shame, representing the result of God's withholding His blessing and favor, or the consequence of hidden sin or rebellion.

Zacharias and Elizabeth were in leadership positions, priests of the Tabernacle, serving according to their order. Zacharias served in the Abijah class of priest. There were 24 such classes, each serving one week in the Temple two times a year. Elizabeth belonged to the descendants of Aaron, Israel's past high priest. Zacharias, a priest, had married a direct descendant of the priestly line, thus attaining a "double-dignity identification" distinction. Added to the fact that they not only held religious positions with the best of family distinction, was the truth that they were also genuinely godly, humble and righteous in all ways. They were the perfect couple for God to shower His blessings upon, but Scripture says, "They were without child, Elizabeth was barren."

Moving from the Knowledge-Part to the God-Part

The name Zacharias means "the Lord remembers"[3]; Elizabeth's name means "my God is an absolutely faithful one," or "my God is an oath."[4] Zacharias and Elizabeth had decided to trust God as the faithful God who remembers all His promises to us and for us. They were not moved by their barrenness and had no knowledge of why barrenness prevailed in their marriage.

The Elizabeth Factor describes those ministries or churches that have done everything they know to be fruitful, successful and influential in a righteous manner, yet without apparent results. Understanding church-growth principles, evangelism ideas, and how to have a successful church are only part of the true picture. There is also the God-part, the hidden part, the sovereign will of God being worked out quietly and secretly. The timetable is in God's hands; the purpose of God is to be fulfilled in the fullness of time.

A church may be without numerical growth and still be blessed and used of God while having no hidden sins to deal with. A church may also be barren because of its poor leadership, violations of basic New Testament principles, hidden wickedness or failure to handle the generation slippage. Barrenness may be God-sent and God-allowed, or it may be caused by obvious spiritual flaws. The Elizabeth Factor, however, is when churches are doing most things well (good leadership, fervent prayer, righteous behavior, honoring God in humility, relevant cultural methodology) and yet are not seeing the desired growth: "There are no new converts or very few converts in our church. Year after year we can't break the 100-people barrier (or the 500-people barrier or the 1,000-people barrier). I'm doing everything I know to do, and there is still an invisible wall!"

The Elizabeth Factor unfolds what is behind the scenes in God's timing for certain breakthroughs and what we can do if we face a similar set of circumstances.

When Time is Working Against You

The advanced age of the couple removes all hope of ever having a child: "Both well advanced in years" (Luke 1:7). Biological birth is now humanly impossible. In the childbearing years it was simply, "Lord, when will You do for us what is normal, possible and within the scope of life?" Now, however, it is in the realm of the impossible and abnormal. A miracle is needed. The timing factor of God's dealings, provisions and answers to prayer is absolutely unpredictable and unexplainable.

Have you given your best years to a ministry or a church only to realize that your time has run out? It's gone, history, never to be repeated. It's over. All those years of serving, preaching, sacrificing, proving and believing, and now the years have come and gone without the vision being fulfilled. Are you close to the age of retirement? Are you moving from your 40s to your 50s, realizing that the many things you have dreamed about are almost—if not for sure—impossible now? Are you well advanced in years in comparison to what you desire to see and what you actually have? Did you set high and lofty goals according to the age chart and find yourself falling behind, so far behind now that it is an impossibility to fulfill those goals? Have you, like me, hung slogans to inspire you such as Charles Paul Conn's from his book *Making It Happen?*

Whatever it is
However impossible it sounds
Whatever the obstacle that lies between you and it
If it is noble
If it is consistent with God's kingdom
You must hunger after it and stretch yourself to reach it.[5]

Yet now do you find that what inspired you when you first posted these motivating lines works the opposite on your soul? Guilty. Frustrated. Failure. No time left!

I never wanted to accept the status quo. I always desired God's best, the highest goal, the achiever's mind-set. J. B. Phillips paraphrases Philippians 1:10: "I want you to be able always to recognize the highest and the best." I have tried to press toward the mark of the high calling, setting high goals with excellence as a hallmark. But now, time has run out. It would take a miracle for me to accomplish what I thought to be a God-vision.

This is the Elizabeth Factor: well advanced in years. Time is working against you every day. "I'm over the hill. Time is not on my side." Take heart. Remember: Benjamin Franklin was 81 years old when he helped to create the Constitution of the United States; George Bernard Shaw was 94 when one of his plays was first performed; Golda Meir was 71 when she was elected Prime Minister of Israel!

Divine Interruptions During Routine Ministry

The class to which Zacharias belonged was having its regular week of priestly service in the sanctuary: "So it was, that while he was serving as priest before God in the order of his division" (Luke 1:8). This priestly service was rendered by Zacharias with faithfulness, respect to God and respect to his calling as a priest. According to the custom of the priesthood, his "lot" fell to burn incense. It was the custom to cast lots for this highest daily task of burning the incense on the golden altar in the holy place. Only once in a priest's life could he be granted this high privilege.

The priest would sprinkle frankincense upon the coals, causing a cloud to arise, spreading fragrance. He then prostrated himself with his face to the ground. His task was the symbolic representation of the rising up to God of the prayers and longings of the people. The priest would then, while the incense cloud was present, offer up prayers consisting of thanksgiving for blessings received and supplication for the peace of Israel. The people who gathered outside the Temple would at the same time prostrate themselves and offer prayers.

The divine interruption happened while Zacharias performed his sacred duties as he had been performing for more than 30 years. For more than 30 years nothing supernatural had happened, and there was nothing extraordinary about his ministry or his name. He was simply one of hundreds who performed their religious duties. His wife would be supportive at every event, every day, every moment to her husband's calling as a faithful priest. Barrenness did not hinder their service unto God, even in the mundane that was more boring than exciting, more habit than adventure. But all that would change in an unsolicited interruption. They were not expecting a visitation from an angel and a proclamation of a miracle child.

The lot fell to Zacharias that day as a custom was being performed. Behind the custom was the invisible, supernatural, sovereign hand of God fulfilling His purposes in Zacharias and Elizabeth's lives. The extraordinary hand of God moved in the ordinary circumstances of life.

When barrenness and time are against you, you must keep doing the things God has already given you to do.

It is important to grasp that when barrenness and time are against you, you must keep doing the things God has already given you to do. Keep preaching, keep praying, keep serving, keep sacrificing, keep overseeing. For in the routine, the mundane, the normal, the common, the everyday events will be a supernatural intervention. The key is commitment in the normal, commitment in the common, commitment to burn incense for the people whether your prayers are answered or not.

The timing of God in answering our prayers is more in step with His purposes than we might know. In God's hidden purposes, a forerunner would be summoned and sent before the long-awaited Messiah: "But the angel said to him '...your petition has been heard, and your wife Elizabeth will bear you a son'" (v. 13, *NASB*). The forerunner would be the fulfillment of Old Testament prophecy and would hold a high and lofty position in God's kingdom.

The need for the forerunner and the miracle Zacharias and Elizabeth desired would meet together at the intersection of divine timing. Elizabeth and Zacharias had hoped for a child in days gone by, but only a child, not a special child. Any child would have satisfied them. But their days of childbearing had been put behind them. The petitions they had offered many years ago had ended with their season of natural childbearing. A biological child was impossible now...or so it appeared in the natural!

Zacharias was now burning incense and offering prayers for the nation. Surprise! Prayers are often effectively heard by God long before He sends the answer. This was God's timing—the time He selected to grant all those fervent petitions of years past. More than grant them, God would combine with their granting the beginnings of the fulfillment of the Messianic Hope.[6] God's timing brought a divine sense of purpose, provision and promise—far greater than Elizabeth and Zacharias could ever have imagined.

The bands of barrenness were broken by a supernatural visitation of God. The school of barrenness once again produced a God-ordained powerful ministry that would be used by God to accomplish His kingdom purposes. The waiting, the pain, the humiliation all vanished as the word of the Lord was received and fulfilled.

Press on, fellow Christian, your bands of barrenness will break, and when they do, your destiny will collide with His timing to produce more than you expected for a purpose that will far exceed the hope of your petitions past.

Lessons from the School of Barrenness

In this chapter we have discovered that:

- The proper combination for healthy church growth is the power of God and the responsibility of man.
- Trusting His sovereignty is realizing that our timetable is in God's hands.
- Many who have gone before us have experienced their greatest achievements in the last lap of their lives.
- When barrenness and time are against you, you must keep doing the things God has already given you to do. God interrupts those who are faithful in the routine and mundane with supernatural interventions.

- "Impossible" is just a word. God will not be constrained by man's word, rather He fulfills His own Word in His time for His kingdom purposes.
- When God breaks the bands of barrenness, our destinies far exceed our petitions past.

((Making It Personal))

1. Can you identify with Zacharias and Elizabeth? Do your goals and dreams seem to have surpassed their season of fruition? Will you keep looking to God?
2. Do you feel as though life has passed you by? If so, has the story of Zacharias and Elizabeth convinced you that God can still burst forth into your ordinary circumstances with a baton of victory you never expected to carry?
3. In what ways have you developed attitudes that are resistant to serving in the mundane, routine and even boring tasks of ministry?
4. Do others look to you as a "Zacharias/Elizabeth" model of faithfulness? If not, will you choose to change?

Notes

1. Robert K. Hudnut, *Churcn Growth Is Not the Point* (N.Y.: HarperCollins, 1975), p. 33.
2. R. C. H. Lenski, *Lenski's Commentary* (Minneapolis: Augsburg Publishing House, 1946), p. 39.
3. G. W. Bromiley, Editor, *International Standard Bible Encyclopedia Vol. 4* (Grand Rapids, William B. Eerdman, 1982), p. 1182.
4. Ibid., p. 73.
5. Charles Paul Conn, *Making It Happen* (from a magazine article).
6. R. C. H. Lenski, *Lenski's Commentary on St. Luke's Gospel* (Minneapolis: Augsburg Publishing House, 1946), p. 45.

12

Michal: Lessons About Despising Attitudes

◡

Pursue peace with all people, and holiness, without
which no one will see the Lord: looking carefully
lest anyone fall short of the grace of God;
lest any root of bitterness springing up cause
trouble, and by this many become defiled.

—*Hebrews 12:14,15*

Barrenness may be allowed to accomplish God's work in God's
way, in God's time; thus He receives all the glory for His wisdom
and His power to fulfill His purposes. God-allowed barrenness is
usually temporary and seasonal; it has a set time to be broken.
There is also a barrenness that may be the result of certain acts
of human failure or satanic harassment. This barrenness may be
remedied if the cause is found and corrected. The principle of
"human negligence" barrenness is alluded to in 2 Peter 1:8:

For if these things are yours and abound, you will be neither barren nor unfruitful in the knowledge of our Lord
Jesus Christ.

Because of the new birth and the promises associated with it,
Christians participate in the divine nature, but the new birth does
not rule out human activity. Spiritual growth and fruitfulness
involve a work of God in which the believer cooperates: a part-
nership.[1] This verse encourages the principle of human responsibility coupled with God's divine power and promises to produce
fruitfulness.

Negligence is a barrenness that is simply the result of a lack of
discipline, determination and active faith. We are to make every
effort to fulfill God's Word over us and in us to become fruitful
both in our ministries and in our churches. The Scripture exhorts
believers not to be lazy, idle or barren (see Matt. 12:36; 20:3,6;
1 Tim. 5:13; Titus 1:12; Jas. 2:20).

Barrenness Assured:
Despising What God Loves

Second Samuel 6:12-23 records the story of when King David
restored the Ark of the Covenant to Israel and gives special
insight into the response of David's wife, Michal. Scripture says
that David danced before the Lord with all his might (see v. 14)
with shouting and trumpets (see v. 15). However, when Michal
observed David from her upstairs windows, she despised him in
her heart (see v. 16). Michal's attitude of despising is revealed in
2 Samuel 6:20: "Then David returned to bless his household. And
Michal the daughter of Saul came out to meet David, and said,
'How glorious was the king of Israel today, uncovering himself
today in the eyes of the maids of his servants, as one of the base
fellows shamelessly uncovers himself!'"

Michal was the younger daughter of Saul. Her mother was
Ahinoam. Michal became David's first wife after Saul had vowed
that the man who killed Goliath would become his son-in-law,

but refused to give David his first daughter, Merab. Saul then asked for a dowry of 100 dead Philistines. When David killed 200 Philistines, Saul handed Michal over to David.

Michal, although a princess, does not appear to have had a very commendable character. Desire for prestige, fervor of infatuation, indifference to holiness and idolatry mark out her character. Her despising attitude over her husband David's rejoicing

❂

An attitude of despising what God esteems will open us to the bands of barrenness.

❂

reveals her pride and lack of sensitivity to the worship Jehovah desired. She had no feelings about the return of the sacred Ark of the Covenant to Zion. This callous attitude is a reflection of her heart condition, and this hardness of heart caused her to despise the things of God. The despising resulted in Michal being barren from that day until her death: "Therefore Michal the daughter of Saul had no children to the day of her death" (v. 23). The simple fact is that an attitude of despising what God esteems will open us to the bands of barrenness.

The word "to despise" (Hebrew: *bazah*) as used in Scripture can mean "to abhor, lightly esteem, to scorn, to make vile."[2] The Scripture states specific areas we are to be careful not to despise.

Do Not Despise Davidic Worship

We are not to despise the expression of biblical worship. Worship is highly esteemed by God: He seeks and requests it of His people. God has asked His worshipers to worship with their whole hearts, with full strength and with selfless abandonment. We must be very careful when being exposed to a Davidic kind of worship that we do not despise, abhor or lightly esteem what God has called sacred, blessed and holy. Davidic worship was given in zeal and with emotion, with shamelessness before the presence of God and with God as the focus.

The term "Davidic worship" is used to enclose the whole revelation of participative worship as presented in the Bible, giving special acknowledgment to King David who introduced in the book of Psalms the ways in which the whole of a person can express praise to God: verbal acclamations, singing, praising, shouting, the use of hands in lifting, clapping and playing musical instruments, and even bodily posture and movement as in bowing, standing and dancing. These are the expressions of worship that a Michal attitude despises.

As leaders who have influence with our attitudes and words, we must be careful not to push our own opinions, agendas or emotional concerns onto the people of God in worship. A despising of the biblical style of worship can be the cause for spiritual barrenness in churches. The Scriptures exhort the Church to worship by offering spiritual sacrifices (see 1 Pet. 2:5) with reverence and zeal (see Ps. 69:9; 95:6). Colossians 3:16 reads:

> Let the word of Christ dwell in you richly in all wisdom, teaching and admonishing one another in psalms and hymns and spiritual songs, singing with grace in your hearts to the Lord.

This Scripture exhorts psalms, hymns and spiritual songs. Most churches sing psalms or hymns, but what about spiritual songs, songs of a spontaneous and spiritual nature? What about singing a new song to the Lord, a song of worship, praise and exaltation that is not of man-made origin (see Ps. 40:3; 144:9; 1 Cor. 14:26)? A true spirit of worship may be the power source to break the bands of barrenness of a stagnant, failing church.

Spiritual songs can be defined as songs of praise in a spontaneous or unpremeditated nature that are sung under the impetus of the Holy Spirit (see Eph. 5:19; Col. 3:16). There are 85 specific places in Scripture that exhort the Church to sing praises to God (see Ps. 47:6; 68:8,17; 98:9). Scripture indicates that praise offered to God in a biblical fashion will bring mighty and supernatural results. Let's consider some of the benefits to sincere praise and worship:

- Praise and worship breaks spiritual bondages (see 1 Sam. 16:23).
- Praise and worship brings spiritual victory (see Hos. 2:14-18).
- Praise and worship uplifts the defeated spirit (see Ps. 25:1; Isa. 61:3).
- Praise and worship brings the presence of the Lord (see 2 Chron. 5:13,14).
- Praise and worship releases the prophetic word (see 2 Kings 3:11-16; 1 Sam. 10:5,6,10).

Do Not Despise the Prophetic Gifts

We are not to despise the use of prophetic gifts in the Church. A comparative look at 1 Thessalonians 5:20 in both the *New King James Version* and the *New International Version* gives us a clearer understanding of the need for this exhortation:

Do not despise prophecies (*NKJV*).
Do not treat prophecies with contempt (*NIV*).

Apparently the Christians at Thessalonica, like those at Corinth (see 1 Cor. 14:1), had underrated the gift of prophecy. The directive may literally be translated, "Stop treating prophecies with contempt." Certain "idle" believers had obviously misused this gift by falsifying data regarding the Lord's return. These counterfeit utterances had soured the remainder of the flock against prophecy in general, so their tendency was not to listen to any more prophetic messages, but to discount them in view of counterfeit utterances they had heard.[3]

By making light of prophetic utterances, these members missed the edification, encouragement and consolation brought by the prophetic ministry. Moreover, by despising the prophetic utterances, their giver—the Holy Spirit—was being dishonored. In the Early Church, the gift of prophesying was like a mighty burning flame. It was not to be quenched or extinguished (see Matt. 12:2; 25:8; Mark 9:48; Eph. 6:16; Heb. 11:34).[4]

A church desiring to break the bands of barrenness must not despise the gifts of the Spirit, especially the gift of prophecy. And yet because there has been so much excess, abuse and counterfeit usage of prophecy, many churches do not accept it as an authentic gift for today's church. If indeed it is a gift of the Spirit, fueled by the Spirit and a voice of the Spirit, we would indeed be quenching the Holy Spirit by quenching prophecy.

New Testament prophecy is not the same as New Testament preaching. Two different Greek words are used with two different results. Prophecy grows out of the moving, ecstatic experience of being overcome by God's Spirit in such a way that words spoken while in the Spirit come not from reflection and study, but solely from God for the edification of the Church. Preaching is a studious approach to a subject followed by a speech of presentation.

Prophecy is a great companion and a wonderful complement to preaching. Prophecy is to build up the Church, to make great stated truths of Scripture become personalized and real in a given setting. True prophecy does not contradict or replace Scripture at any time. It submits to and is judged by Scripture (see Rom. 12:6-8; 1 Cor. 12:8-10; 14:1-6,26-32; Eph. 4:11; 1 Thess. 5:19-22).[5] We are not to cast away or despise the words spoken with the use of the prophetic gifts. There is power for deliverance, encouragement, vision and spiritual brokenness when this gift is allowed. Barren churches may need to reevaluate the use of prophecy and other spiritually powerful tools for building the church (see Ps. 50:17; Isa. 5:24; Jer. 6:10; Num. 15:31; 2 Chron. 3:16).

Do Not Despise the Chastening of the Lord

In Hebrews 12:5,6 we are exhorted not to despise the God-sent correction of the Lord:

And you have forgotten the exhortation which speaks to you as to sons: "My son, do not despise the chastening of the Lord, nor be discouraged when you are rebuked by Him; for whom the Lord loves He chastens, and scourges every son whom He receives."

Ministries and churches at times will receive the correction of the Lord through a rebuke, a chastisement through circumstances, or people used to correct something we would rather not look at. A resistance to God-sent correction will ultimately confer a hardness of heart and result in spiritual stagnation and barrenness.

The word "discipline" combines the thoughts of chastening and education. It points to sufferings that teach us the ways of God. No circumstances are beyond God's sovereign control, and there are none He cannot use to carry out His purposes. Leaders and churches are not to belittle this powerful tool in breaking the bands of barrenness. Could it be that a leader's self-will, pride or ego-driven style of leadership is the band of barrenness on the church?

God in His love and wisdom will bring chastisement through circumstances, people or other ministries to humble and deliver such a leader. Chastening keeps us from becoming wayward prodigal sons. Chastening may be:

Preventative: as with Paul's thorn in the flesh;
Corrective: which is administering discipline as with John Mark;
Enlarging: as in King David's time in the wilderness in caves being harassed by King Saul;
Breaking: a divine conquering of the human will so a total yielding to God will be accomplished.

If we want to break the bands of barrenness, we must not neglect the attitudes of our hearts. We must refuse to despise those things that stretch us and cause us to lay down our rigidity. We must be pliable to God's dealings with us, realizing that holy hearts are the incubators for the fulfilled purposes and promises of our Holy God.

Lessons from the School of Barrenness

In this chapter we have discovered that:

- Negligence is a barrenness that is simply the result of a lack of discipline, determination and active faith. We are not to be idle or lazy.
- When our hearts become callous toward the things of God, we open ourselves to barrenness.
- A true spirit of worship may be the power source to break the bands of barrenness of a stagnant, failing church.
- When we despise the prophetic giftings, we quench the Holy Spirit and deny His power for deliverance, encouragement, vision and spiritual brokenness.
- A leader's self-will, pride or ego-driven style of leadership can be the band of barrenness on the church. Chastisement is God's remedy for such leaders.
- We must embrace God's discipline, knowing that it will be used to break our bands of barrenness.

(((Making It Personal)))

1. Have you fallen into the trap of laziness or lack of zeal for the things of God? If so, what steps are you willing to take to reverse your attitude?
2. Is your worship reflective of a heart that is abandoned to God, or is it restrained by the fear of outward appearances?
3. In what ways have you attempted to restrict the Holy Spirit in your ministry or church? Are you open to the prophetic giftings?
4. Can you think of any people or circumstances God has sent to chasten you that have caused you to harden your heart? In what ways do you need to be more pliable?

Notes

1. Frank Gabelein, *Expositor's Bible Commentary Vol. 12* (Grand Rapids: Zondervan, 1995), p. 269.
2. *BDB*, p. 102; *TWOT* #224.
3. Frank Gabelein, *Expositor's Bible Commentary Vol. 11* (Grand Rapids: Zondervan, 1995), p. 293.
4. William Hendrickson, *New Testament Commentary: Thessalonians, Timothy, Titus* (Grand Rapids: Baker Book House), p. 140.
5. For further information from the author's viewpoint, refer to his book *The Prophetic Ministry* (Portland, Oreg.: Trilogy Productions, Inc., 1983).

13

Diseased Spiritual Rivers

ↄ

And it shall be that every living thing that moves,

wherever the rivers go, will live.

—*Ezekiel 47:9*

When Israel continued in a backslidden condition, breaking God's laws and abandoning God's covenant, not listening to the prophets or responding to God's correction, God would speak heavy and corrective words to His adulterous wife:

> As for Ephraim, their glory shall fly away like a bird—no birth, no pregnancy, and no conception!...Give them, O Lord—what will You give? Give them a miscarrying womb and dry breasts! (Hos. 9:11,14).

The judgment passed on to Israel was a miscarrying womb, barrenness. This judgment was not God's desire for Israel. Rather, barrenness was Israel's consequence for a continued path of rebellion, lukewarmness and blatant disobedience to God's ways. God had promised the blessing of offspring when His Word and ways were respected. (Exod. 23:26: "No one shall suffer miscarriage or be barren in your land; I will fulfill the number of your days." Deut. 7:14: "You shall be blessed above all peoples; there shall not be a male or female barren among you or among your livestock.") When the blessing of God was evident, no barrenness existed in the animals, the land or the family. But when God's people turned from His covenant, His Word and His ways, His judgment was implemented through the curse of barrenness.

Barrenness Within Our Churches

All ministries and churches desire God's divine blessings. We desire spiritual fruit, growth and influence. We desire to influence our cities, our nation, our world. Yet our desires are met with limitations, obstacles, bondages and resistance. Obviously the enemy of God and the Church, the devil, does not wish our success. He works against the Church with every weapon and scheme possible for our defeat. But God is our shield and buckler, a mighty warrior. He fights for us with His weapons, which are far superior to those of our enemy. Yet even with God on our side, we still seem to be so slow, so pitiful, so limited in our outreach and influence. Why?

Not all our barrenness problems are with the devil. At times our problems stem from within. A stagnated spiritual life could be the result of breaking covenant with God, faulty leadership or a diseased spiritual river.

Barren Leaders, Barren Churches

Barrenness in the life of the leader will certainly be a contributing factor to the barrenness in the life of the local church. A spiritually dried up leader will contribute to the lack of spiritual conception, pregnancy and birth. A barren leader may hinder the church by not stepping aside and allowing others to take the church further. The leader may hinder the church by embracing doctrinal extremes, leaning toward the obscurity of Scripture rather than its simplicity. Doctrinal extremes can be evidenced in a continued focus on Old Testament typology and prophecy that are misinterpreted and misapplied.

The obsession for some new doctrine or new twist on an old doctrine instead of the sure foundation of God's Word can keep a church in a miscarrying state for years at a time. Some churches never break these bands of barrenness. They are always blaming barrenness on some perceived satanic attack, spiritual stronghold or some problem in the congregation that is hindering fruitfulness: *It's the people, the city, the state, the country, the sin of someone, the hard-heartedness or shallowness of the people.*

Leaders who lead out of a barren ministry usually produce a barren church. They perpetuate a string of miscarriages by refusing to step aside, embracing doctrinal extremes, creating structural frailty within the church, compromising through moral weakness, neglecting vision and planning, and succumbing to impulsive decisions. This lack of healthy leadership creates a spiritual dilemma. The church continues to conceive, carrying vision for a time, but then loses the baby.

Miscarrying churches are frustrating for everyone involved, and the search for causes can become bizarre. When different people with different perspectives, and different levels of spiritual maturity and motivation disagree on the causes, great division and discord can erupt.[1]

Diseased Spiritual Rivers

Another cause of spiritual barrenness is a diseased spiritual river within the church:

> Then the men of the city said to Elisha, "Please notice, the situation of this city is pleasant, as my lord sees; but the water is bad, and the ground barren." And he said, "Bring me a new bowl, and put salt in it." So they brought it to him. Then he went out to the source of the water, and cast in the salt there, and said, "Thus says the Lord: 'I have

healed this water; from it there shall be no more death or barrenness'" (2 Kings 2:19-21).

The barren land was connected to the barren water, water that needed healing. This diseased water was able to cast death into the land and barrenness into the crops. It was water, but it was sick water. Every local church has a spiritual life flow that we may call "the river of God" in that church.

The river of God is the spiritual flow caused by Holy Spirit activity in and around present truths and, at times, is affected by seasonal outpourings of God's presence. During revival seasons God pours out His Spirit as rain, as water upon dry ground, as rivers in the desert. The river of God should be a river of life, health, healing and power. It should bring with it fruitfulness, not barrenness.

In Ezekiel 47:1-12, the river symbolically flowed from the Temple, a river that we are to swim in, enjoy and preserve. Ezekiel's vision of the river described a man moving into the river, first to his ankles (v. 3), then to his knees (v. 4), then to his waist (v. 4), and finally into water too deep to walk in, so he had to launch out and swim (v. 5). It was a river that could not be crossed. As the vision continued, the power of the river was witnessed. The vision shows what happens when the river comes.

Evidence of a Healthy Spiritual River

The magnificence of the river is seen in its great power to bring life not death, healing not sickness, growth not stagnation, multitudes not smallness, world outreach not ingrownness (see Ezek. 47:7; Ps. 1:1-6; Isa. 61:1-4). The river of God in our churches is to be like the river in Ezekiel's vision:

The river is a place for many trees to be planted (v. 7).
The river reaches to the eastern regions (v. 8).
The river flows down into every valley (v. 8).
The river brings healing to the waters (v. 9).

The river causes life to spring forth everywhere (v. 9).
The river has a great multitude of fish (v. 9).
The river causes healing and health to everything (v. 9).
The river will be a place for net fishing (v. 10).
The river will minister healing to the nations (v. 12).
The river will produce very fruitful trees (v. 12).

The late Peter Marshall, an eloquent speaker, and for several years the chaplain of the United States Senate, loved to tell the story of "The Keeper of the Spring," a quiet forest dweller who lived high above an Austrian village along the eastern slopes of the Alps. The old gentleman had been hired many years ago by a young town council to clear away the debris from the pools of water up in the mountain crevices that fed the lovely spring flowing through its town. With faithful, silent regularity, the old man patrolled the hills, removed the leaves and branches, and wiped away the silt that would otherwise choke and contaminate the fresh flow of water. By and by, the village became a popular attraction for vacationers. Graceful swans floated along the crystal clear spring, the mill wheels of various businesses located near the water turned day and night, farmlands were naturally irrigated, and the view from restaurants was picturesque beyond description.

Years passed. One evening the town council met for its semiannual meeting. As the council members reviewed the budget, one man's eye caught the figure for the salary being paid the obscure Keeper of the Spring. Said the keeper of the purse, "Who is the old man? Why do we keep him on year after year? No one ever sees him. For all we know the strange ranger of the hills is doing us no good. He isn't necessary any longer!" By a unanimous vote, they dispensed with the old man's services.

For several weeks nothing changed. By early autumn the trees began to shed their leaves. Small branches snapped off and fell into the pools, hindering the rushing flow of sparkling water. One afternoon someone noticed a slight yellowish-brown tint in the spring. A couple days later the water appeared much darker. Within another week, a slimy film covered sections of the water along the banks and a foul odor was soon detected. The mill wheels moved slower, some finally ground to a halt. Swans left, as did the tourists. Clammy fingers of disease and sickness reached deeply into the village.

Quickly, the embarrassed council called a special meeting. Realizing their gross error in judgment, they hired back the old Keeper of the Spring...and within a few weeks the veritable river

We must see to it that we don't stagnate through lack of worship and intimacy with the Father [or]...become polluted with unbalanced teaching or impure motives and attitudes.

of life began to clear up. The wheels started to turn, and new life returned to the hamlet in the Alps once again.[2]

Fanciful though it may be, the story is more than an idle tale. It carries with it a vivid, relevant analogy relating to the river of God in our lives and churches. At times barrenness is a human-induced problem, at other times a judgment of God for violations of God's ordained laws. The point is that we must keep watch over our spiritual lives. We must see to it that we don't stagnate through lack of worship and intimacy with the Father. We must see to it that the rivers do not become polluted with unbalanced teaching or impure motives and attitudes. We must keep our spiritual waters free from the logjams of unforgiveness and allow the freshness of His love to pour in and through us at all times.

The Subtle Swamps in the Midst of Revival

We must also be alerted to a subtle potential death that can occur right in the middle of revival, during a time of rain and power—the swamps and marshes: "But its swamps and marshes will not be healed; they will be given over to salt" (Ezek. 47:11).

The potential swamps and marshes in the local church that have the capability of destroying the power of God's river are the low grounds filled with water, causing the ground to become nonproductive because of continual wetness. This marshland or boggy ground has no way to drain or become solid ground, so it becomes diseased, sick, bug infested, putrid and dangerous. God desires a river not a swamp, a flow not a bog.

A church that lingers too long in the waters of revival without investing in proper teaching, sound doctrine, family building and character shaping will eventually turn into a swamp. God desires that our waters be healed, that our rivers be pure and that our spiritual flow not be mixed or compromised. He wants us to enjoy the fresh rain of revival, but He also wants us to be rooted as trees that are grounded in the basics of His truth.

The River of God—From Genesis to Revelation

God has always used rivers as a symbol of His life-giving Spirit. From Genesis to Revelation we see examples of His desire to touch people through the rivers that flow between the pages of His Word:

The river in the garden (see Gen. 2:10).
The river in the city (see Ps. 46:4).
The river in the wilderness (see Josh. 3:1,2,14,15).
The river in the Temple (see Ezek. 47:1-12).
The river in the believer (see John 7:37-39).
The river from His throne (see Rev. 22:1).

God desires that every church have a healthy river, a place of passing through new spiritual experiences and a place of encountering a new flow of spiritual life, power and blessings. This river signifies a divine spiritual life force that waters the people of God through His rich and ever-enduring presence. There is a river of God that is encouraged by obeying God's proven principles and patterns.

There is also a river that speaks of a spiritual flow and Holy Spirit activity within the context of revival—healing, power and fresh anointing all mixed together and flowing without human initiative or human control. We step into the river by hungering and thirsting after Him. Like healing minerals, God's supernatural power becomes evident and we are refreshed, cleansed and healed by the river.

Healing the Diseased River

A church may have a stagnant river, a mixed or weak flowing river, a shallow or dead river, a destroying out-of-control river, or a religious river filled with form and tradition but no real life. Whatever the case, God desires to heal your waters and to bring new life and health into your river. This healed river will break the bands of barrenness and release a powerful new flow of God upon the church.

God will direct openhearted leaders to know how to bring the needed healing. One person may be told that salt must be cast into the water (see 2 Kings 2:21). Salt speaks of the power of preservation and penetration through the Spirit of the new covenant, returning to the sure blessing of sound doctrine.

Another leader might be directed by the Spirit to cast a tree into the water as in Exodus 15:23 and 25: "Now when they came to Marah, they could not drink the waters of Marah, for they were bitter....So he [Moses] cried out to the Lord." Our part in healing the waters is to cry unto the Lord, to beg Him for insight, spiritual perspective, a word for this present pool of bitter waters. What will bring the healing? What will stop the barrenness?

"And the Lord showed him..." (v. 25). This is your hope and your ground of intercession. The Lord will show you the specific act of healing for *your* waters. It will not be the same as that of other leaders or churches. It will not be the same for you the next time the waters need healing. But for now, for this Marah, for this bitter water, He will show you what you should do:

> And the Lord showed him a tree. When he cast it into the waters, the waters were made sweet (v. 25).

For Moses it was a tree. For Elisha it was the salt. Each had power because each had received the word of the Lord for that moment and for that specific sick water or river. God delights in speaking to His leaders and "showing them" what they need to cast into the waters. The healed river will be like the river in Revelation 22:1: "And he showed me a pure river of water of life, clear as crystal, proceeding from the throne of God and of the Lamb."

The land will bear much fruit when the water is healed. There will be no barrenness, no miscarriage, no lack of fruitfulness, but a springing forth with much fruit. Rise up, leader of God, and step into the water.

Lessons from the School of Barrenness

In this chapter we have discovered that:

- A stagnated spiritual life could be the result of breaking covenant with God, faulty leadership or a diseased spiritual river.
- Extremes in doctrine can lead us away from the truth and cause us to enter a season of barrenness.
- The river of God is the flow of God in a church or ministry. Lack of worship and intimacy with the Father will stagnate the water.
- A church that lingers too long in the waters of revival without investing in proper teaching, sound doctrine, family building and character shaping will eventually turn into a swamp.
- The answer to diseased spiritual waters is to call out to God through intercession. The Lord will show you the specific act of healing for your waters.

((Making It Personal))

1. How healthy are the waters of your spiritual life? How much time are you spending in private worship with the heavenly Father?

2. What kind of leadership do you bring to your church or ministry? Is your teaching balanced? Are you given to impulsiveness rather than vision and planning? Is the internal structure of your church healthy enough to survive without you?

3. Are you open to a fresh anointing from God? Where do the waters of your spiritual life need to be stirred? In what ways have you become stagnated?

Notes

1. For further study in these areas, see *Making of a Leader* (Portland, Oreg.: Bible Temple Publishing, 1987-1988) and *Vanguard Leadership* (Portland, Oreg.: Bible Temple Publishing, 1994) both by Frank Damazio.

2. Although I was not able to locate this quotation by Peter Marshall, I do want to make sure that he receives credit for it.

14

The Secret to New Life

◑

He died for all, that those who live should live

no longer for themselves, but for Him who

died for them and rose again.

—*2 Corinthians 5:15*

Our Bible college was beginning its last week of spring semester, a very busy week with year-end activities. The main event, of course, was the graduation ceremony, the final honoring of students who had paid the price to finish a two-year or four-year journey. Our college campus is adjacent to our church campus because it is a church-related Bible college. (I am both the pastor of the church and the president of the college.)

For 30 years we have been training leaders through our college with graduates who now pastor churches, teach in colleges, serve as missionaries on several continents and return as international students to their home countries to pioneer churches and colleges in their own nations. The college trains about 300 full-time students each year. It is a challenging vision.

A New Idea, A New Tradition

I was scheduled to be the graduation speaker for this particular graduating class, so my heart and mind were focused on making this a meaningful experience to reflect on for these young leaders in the years to come. I decided on something that had never been done before, at least not in our college, nor had I heard of it done elsewhere. But it was burning in my spirit as the right symbolic act for this graduation ceremony. I had no idea I would be establishing a tradition; I had only desired to do it one time, for this class.

I had decided to conduct the ceremony during the second or main service on Sunday morning. For years it had been held on a Sunday evening, more of a college event without the majority of the church attending. But this changed everything. The church would be the backdrop for this event as the college led the prayer, worship and special music. The chemistry of the two joined at this graduation was very powerful and meaningful.

The church now bore witness to the fruit of the labor and promise for the future of these world leaders. The stage was set as I stood to take my turn at the podium. I must admit that I was a little apprehensive about how my symbolic act would be received. First, I presented my message: a biblical explanation of what I was about to do. Then, I presented each student with a piece of wood—a stick, a miniature of Aaron's rod with his or her name engraved on it.

I stepped before each graduate, handing that person a dead piece of wood, a barren rod with no sign of life, fruitfulness or supernatural visitation. It was just a piece of dead wood with that graduate's name on it and a prayer: "May your life ministry become a living rod. May it bud and bring forth supernatural fruit. May it not remain a dead piece of wood." The atmosphere was heavy with God's presence and a feeling of being suspended in time and space.

We were standing in the presence of God with a glimpse into our future, a small token in our hands that helped us to reach out with faith and say, "O God, please let my rod be transformed from a dead piece of wood into a fruitful, supernatural rod."

Tears were shed and hearts were touched deeply. It was one of those few times in life during which words spoken would have seemed superficial in comparison to the holiness of the experience—we were standing on holy ground. It was a divine moment; God was choosing His leaders.

God's Direction for the Selection of Leaders

God has always been concerned with the selection of leaders. Numbers 17 presents the final vindication of the Lord's confidence in His selection of Aaron as the leader of His choice. As Aaron's life reached its end, God made certain that there was no question about His choice of Aaron and his sons. Aaron had four sons. Two were killed by God because of their arrogance and disrespect to His word. Leviticus 10 simply says they offered up strange fire and God killed them. Aaron's other two sons, Eleazar and Ithamar, were to become the twin lines of the priesthood of Israel throughout their generations.

Numbers 17, the rod chapter, establishes several important presuppositions concerning God's ways and means for ministry. God has established ministry to:

- Vindicate most forcibly the right to decide who should be the chosen leadership for His specific work.
- Stop all murmuring and questioning of those who would desire a leadership position not given them by God, and silence murmuring against those who have the position.
- Establish the truth that true ministry is a supernatural achievement in one's life.

The Leader, the Rod

All leaders seeking to be used of God in a significant fashion can be called a rod. All ministries will go through the rod test, the test of barrenness or fruitfulness.

The word "rod" itself has rich meaning both linguistically and conceptually. A rod is a branch, so called from its stretching or extending itself. A rod or staff was used for walking and used for shepherding, chastising and snake killing. As the scepter of a king, it was an emblem of power. A rod was made of very hard wood, sunbaked, weather-beaten, desert wood such as acacia, often gnarled, knotted, twisted, rough and aged.

Historic Significance of the Rod

The historic significance of the rod can be seen both in Scripture and tradition. The rod of the father was handed down from one generation to another. The family would mark the rod with its own family symbols that would identify the family with the rod. The rod came to represent a person's social status, financial prosperity and authority. When borne by the man who was entitled to carry it, the rod was to be respected, thus making the command of Jehovah to Moses of even greater significance: "And the Lord spoke to Moses saying" (Num. 17:1).

The phrase "And the Lord spoke to Moses saying" is not just a mechanical grouping of words for a story transition, not just a stylistic device used in other stories or narrative sections. These words indicate the divine mind flowing to Moses. This phrase is used more than 150 times in Numbers. Jehovah has spoken. This is God's wisdom; it is God's principles stated, God's way established. The rod test was a divine word of wisdom from Jehovah and was to be explicitly followed:

Speak to the children of Israel, and get from them a rod from each father's house, all their leaders according to their fathers' houses—twelve rods. Write each man's name on his rod. And you shall write Aaron's name on the rod of Levi. For there shall be one rod for the head of each father's house (Num. 17:2,3).

Divine Election of Individuals

The rods were to be made very personal by the engraving of each man's name upon the wood. There would be no mistake, no error in discerning which barren rod belonged to which man. The man was to be one with his rod.

God calls and shapes each ministry individually, not collectively. You are who you are by your own choices, character disciplines, pursuits, passions and dreams. Your family tree, your church, your college, your seminary does not determine your future. It is you who decides your future. God calls and equips leaders with special endowments, but ultimately your destiny is

❁

God's call reaches out of eternity. His purpose and actions stem from before the world began.... Barrenness is never God's ultimate calling.

❁

the result of your response, preparation and yielding your rod to God. The Lord calls you by name, a divine selection by God's divine grace and wisdom: "O Lord, You have searched me and known me" (Ps. 139:1).

According to Genesis 12:2, we are not chosen based on our own merits or qualifications. Ours is a calling of grace. God promised Abraham, "I will bless you and make your name great." God's elect are personally foreknown by Him. God does not choose or predestine people as abstract entities, but as real people with real weaknesses and real-life tragedies. God chooses people individually (see Rom. 8:28; 1 Pet. 1:1,2; Eph. 1:4; 2 Thess. 2:13,14). John 15:16 reiterates this fact: "You did not choose Me, but I chose you and appointed you."

Knowing that God has selected us provides an unshakable basis for our call and salvation. God's call reaches out of eternity. His purpose and actions stem from before the world began. God chose and appointed us by name that we should "bear fruit." Barrenness is never God's ultimate calling.

Divine Appointment by Divine Approval

Moses was commanded not only to put each person's name on the rod, but also to place the rods in the Tabernacle of Meeting before the Testimony. Numbers 17:4,5: "Then you shall place them in the tabernacle of meeting before the Testimony, where I meet with you. And it shall be that the rod of the man whom I choose...." Only one rod would receive from the presence of the Lord, the supernatural life resulting in supernatural fruitfulness, a sign of divine approval. Under the same atmosphere, the other rods remained dead, barren pieces of wood. The natural was not changed by the supernatural. The rods were laid before God's sovereignty. The 12 rods were all equal when taken into the Tabernacle of Meeting: all barren, dead pieces of wood. The rods were laid before the Ark of the Covenant, the place of God's awesome presence.

The message is clear, though shrouded in symbolism. The life of the chosen leader is in the life of God's presence. The rod, the leader who will move from barrenness to fruitfulness, is hidden within the veil, meeting God afresh, meeting God through brokenness, contriteness and emptiness. This is the leader who comes with a sense of nothingness, yet is filled and overshadowed by God's overflowing presence.

From Dead Wood to Living Rod

The absence of carnal ambition comes easily when we realize the message of the dead, barren rod. There is nothing we can do to cause life to flow from a dead piece of wood. It is all Him, all God, our source. Our life is hidden in Him. We must nurture a holy ambition, a calling from God to use our gifts in accordance with what He has given us. We ought not withdraw into passivity out of a false sense of humility. Ambition can be a God-given quality that causes people to accomplish things greater than the status quo. Without this God-kind of ambition, we will be less than the people God calls us to be.

The one rod received divine life, resulting in miraculous transformation. Supernatural achievement is the origin of all true ministry. The transformation from dead wood to living rod can only happen as the rod encounters the living presence of the one true and living God. Transformation from natural to supernatural is the work of God and His divine power. Every true ministry is a creation of God, a gift of God to His Church:

> Now it came to pass on the next day that Moses went into the tabernacle of witness, and behold, the rod of Aaron, of the house of Levi, had sprouted and put forth buds, had produced blossoms and yielded ripe almonds (Num. 17:8).

Sprouted. Buds. Blossoms. Ripe almonds. A sprout may come out of a living branch or trunk of a tree, but it is impossible for

☻

When we push outside of our ministry calling, outside of our grace, we will experience barrenness.

☻

a wooden staff that is long dead to sprout again as though it were still part of a growing tree. The sign would be regarded as absolutely and finally convincing, for the hand of God would be impossible for anyone to dispute.

The Reality of Ministry Limitations

As Moses returned from the Tabernacle with the rods in his hands to return them to the owners, it would have been an unusual event. The rods that didn't bud were brought forth and shown to all of Israel. Imagine the awkwardness of Moses as he humbly gave back the dead, barren rods to each man by name. Every man had to embrace the choice of God. Not Moses' choice, not man's choice, but God's choice—God Himself had made the choice:

> Then Moses brought out all the rods from before the Lord to all the children of Israel; and they looked, and each man took his rod (Num. 17:9).

The barren rod was not a personal rejection of the man, but a ministry limitation set by God's grace, mercy and wisdom. When we push outside of our ministry calling, outside of our grace, we will experience barrenness.

Paul accepts his measure, his personal ministry limitation: "We, however, will not boast beyond measure, but within the limits of the sphere which God appointed us—a sphere which especially includes you" (2 Cor. 10:13). The Greek word used here for measure is *metron*, a graduated rod or rule for measuring, that which is measured, a determined extent, a portion measured off (see Rom. 12:3; 2 Cor. 10:13; Eph. 4:7).[1] The gift of grace is measured and given according to the will of God. Whatever the endowment, His is the bestowment and adjustment.[2]

Burnout will also be a possibility when we drive ourselves beyond grace borders. Burnout is an emotional disease of the overcommitted who refuse to come to terms with their ministry limitations. Spiritual burnout may be recognized by the signs of exhaustion, cynicism, irritability, withdrawal, sleeplessness, anxiety, lack of communication and loss of humor.

When we are operating within our calling and gifting, absorbing God's divine presence and divine approval, we experience renewal and are energetic, optimistic, calm, open, creative, competent, communicative with lots of laughter!

Eight Evidences of a Ministry That Is Alive

1. A rod that releases supernatural activity (see Exod. 4:17; 7:19; 8:16; 9:23; 10:13);

2. A rod that releases faith to break through impossible circumstances (see Exod. 14:14-16);
3. A rod that releases spiritual refreshing (see Exod. 17:5; Num. 20:7-9);
4. A rod that releases power to defeat the enemy (see Exod. 17:10-16);
5. A rod that releases spiritual nourishment (see Mic. 7:4);
6. A rod that releases spiritual adjustment (see 1 Cor. 4:21);
7. A rod that releases spiritual authority (see Rev. 2:7; 12:5; 19:15);
8. A rod that releases spiritual vision (see Rev. 11:1,2).

The Divine Preservative of Yielded Rods: God's Grace

The Ark of the Covenant was a place of preservation for the tablets of law (see Exod. 25:21; Deut. 10:5), the golden pot of manna (see Exod. 16:33,34), and Aaron's rod that budded (see Num. 17:10). Hebrews 9:4 says, "...the ark of the covenant overlaid on all sides with gold, in which were the golden pot that had the manna, Aaron's rod that budded, and the tablets of the covenant."

Aaron's rod that budded was to be taken from Aaron and put into the Ark of the Covenant, which was placed in the Most Holy Place. The Tabernacle of Moses had three compartments: the Outer Court, the Holy Place and the Most Holy Place. The Most Holy Place was the place of God's manifest presence, a place where His glory resided. This is where His voice was heard as He spoke to the High Priest from the blood-stained mercy seat, the lid to the Ark of the Covenant. ("And there I will meet with you, and I will speak with you from above the mercy seat, from between the two cherubim which are on the ark of the Testimony, about everything which I will give you in commandment to the children of Israel," Exod. 25:22.)

The rod was to be placed in the Ark of the Covenant to preserve the fruitfulness of the chosen rod. The fruit was to remain forever ripe and never fade. The Ark preserved the rod in unfading beauty. The power of abiding in Christ, abiding in His presence, this is the principle of divine preservation. This is the secret to a long life of fruitfulness: presenting ourselves constantly before His presence because in ourselves we are dry and barren. Our reliance is upon God for our fruitfulness (see Gal. 5:22,23; John 15:1-8).

Whatever we are conscious of, we become eventually occupied with and conquered by. If we keep our ministries in the Ark of Christ's presence, abiding daily in His presence, we will be refreshed with the revelation of God's mind and purpose and endued with fresh anointing. We will be able to refresh others wherever we go. Man's greatest loss in the Fall was God's felt-energizing presence. Divine intimacy produces divine awareness.

A. W. Tozer in his book *The Pursuit of God* states, "As we begin to focus upon God, the things of the Spirit will take shape before our inner eyes. Obedience to the Word of Christ will bring an inward revelation of the Godhead. It will give acute perception, enabling us to see God even as is promised to the pure in heart. A new God-consciousness will seize upon us and we shall begin to taste and hear and inwardly feel God, who is our life and our all. There will be seen the constant shining of 'the true Light, which lighteth every man that cometh into the world' (John 1:9, *KJV*). More and more, as our faculties grow sharper and more sure, God will become to us the great All, and His presence the glory and wonder of our lives."[3]

Lessons from the School of Barrenness

In this chapter we have discovered that:

- God selects leaders. Every leader is a rod called to fulfill a particular branch of ministry in His Church.
- When we recognize that men are appointed by God, we should release our desires for leadership positions not given to us by Him and silence our murmuring

against those who have the positions.

- True ministry is a supernatural achievement in one's life. God is the One who transforms the dead piece of wood into a fruitful, supernatural rod.
- God calls and equips leaders with special endowments, but ultimately your destiny is the result of your response, preparation and yielding your rod to God.
- Barren rods are the result of pushing outside of our ministry calling, outside of our grace boundaries.
- Burnout is an emotional disease of the overcommitted who refuse to come to terms with their ministry limitations.
- We are not chosen based on our own merits or qualifications. Ours is a calling of grace. God will use us in spite of our weaknesses, flaws and circumstances.
- Our rods of ministry will blossom as we empty ourselves in His presence and allow Christ to pour His life through us.

((Making It Personal))

1. In what ways have you been owning your call, your gifts, your ministry? Will you choose to lay down your rod so God can cause it to bloom?
2. Can you think of a leader who holds a position you believe you should have had? Will you make the choice to thank God for His selection?
3. Do you know where your grace borders are? Have you come to terms with the limits God has placed on your ministry?
4. Review the eight qualities of a ministry that is alive. How does your ministry compare?

Notes

1. Walter Bauer, William F. Arndt, F. Wilbur Gingrich and Fredrick W. Banker, *A Greek-English Lexicon of the New Testament and Other Early Christian Literature (Second Edition)*, (Chicago: The University of Chicago Press, 1979; revised from Walter Bauer's fifth edition, 1958), p. 515.

2. W. E. Vine, *Vine's Complete Dictionary of the Old and New Testament* (Nashville: Thomas Nelson Publishers, 1984), p. 399.

3. A. W. Tozer, *The Pursuit of God* (Camp Hill, Pa.: Christian Publications, 1997).

15

Breaking the Unsaved-Unchurched People Barrier

○

When I say to the wicked, "O wicked man,

you shall surely die!" and you do not speak to warn

the wicked from his way, that wicked man shall die in

his iniquity; but his blood I will require at your hand.

Nevertheless if you warn the wicked to turn from his

way, and he does not turn from his way, he shall die

in his iniquity; but you have delivered your soul.

—Ezekiel 33:8,9

I was 26 and Sharon was 23 when we got married in Portland, Oregon, in 1976. In the 21 years of our marriage, we have lived in two cities and five different houses. From 1976 to 1981, I taught

Bible, leadership, communication skills and several other subjects at Portland Bible College. I loved everything about teaching: the students, the challenge of continual research, the students' questions, comments and criticisms....But change was in the wind.

We had decided to plant a new church in Eugene, Oregon, with a small team of 18 people from our college and church. With the pain of the decision-making process, heart-wrenching goodbyes, tears and doubts finally behind us, we arrived in Eugene in January of 1981. We had one month of salary saved, no office, no church building, no promises, and now 25 people who were committed to planting a church. We rented a conference room at the local Holiday Inn and started the church. The journey of transitioning from a teacher in a classroom to a pastor in a rented hotel room would be a new education in itself.

Growing a church is like raising a family. It is the father heart of God loving, reaching, believing and forgiving people. It is not an informational task; it's a transformational one. I soon learned that teaching was a drawing strength for our new church. The only problem is that we were drawing in churched people instead of unchurched people, believers instead of unbelievers. I was simply shifting the Christian population from one building to another. I was not invading hell and releasing spiritually shackled sinners.

From Pastor-Teacher to Pastor-Evangelist

With the passage of time, I changed and the church reflected some of those changes. Moving from teacher to pastor was a spiritually natural process due to the pressures of people's needs and the different environment I lived in daily. But the transition of moving from pastor to pastor-evangelist was much more difficult. This was a challenge, a high mountain to climb without many instructors to help me. A determinative choice was being made, a decision to grow our church both through transplant growth (Christians moving into the city or transferring from other churches—hopefully with their pastors' blessings) and new convert growth.

One form of barrenness churches may experience is seeing only transplant growth or biological growth, not growth through sinners being saved. Breaking the unsaved-people barrier necessitates a strategy for pressing hell to give up souls. Pastors must move from a one-dimensional pastor only (pastor-nurturer or pastor-counselor or pastor-teacher) to a multilevel ministry that includes a pastor-evangelist ministry function.

To criticize seeker-sensitive, evangelistic, soul-seeking churches that are strategically reaching the lost as shallow, compromising and having only temporary influence is truly to miss the whole picture and sidestep the whole challenge. It is not biblical to choose to build the church around a philosophy of ministry that will only reach transplant believers. Sheep swapping is a blind spot in many of our 300,000 American churches, and it also seems to be a global problem.

Penetrating the Unsaved Community

Our aim is the whole gospel for the whole world. Our goal is every person in every people group presented with the gospel before they die. This year in America alone 2.2 million people will die, the majority without ever knowing Christ. There are 262 million people in America and, according to some researchers, 187 million have some conversion understanding. By the thousands we have been praying, fasting and begging for the harvest. Some have had a small taste, others a deep drink of the rivers of revival. Some have tapped into authentic revival. Yet there are thousands of ministries and churches not penetrating the unsaved community. No influence. No salvations. No growth. No spiritual impact. Why?

Several factors seem obvious—from demonic spiritual strongholds to ill-equipped pastors, from finances to traditional and religious bondages and more. The one thing I do know as a pastor who is seeking to break the unsaved people barrier is that we will never break this barrier if we as pastors do not first have a change in our mind, heart, spirit and ministry about our responsibility to be a pastor-evangelist and about releasing our churches into creative, powerful new forms of "city reaching" and "city reaping."

The following Scriptures must first be claimed as we transition into a pastor-evangelist. We must expect the Spirit of the Lord to cover us and make up for our inadequacies.

First, we have the Spirit of the Lord to preach to the lost!

Isaiah 61:1: The Spirit of the Lord God is upon Me, because the Lord has anointed Me to preach good tidings to the poor; He has sent Me to heal the brokenhearted, to proclaim liberty to the captives, and the opening of the prison to those who are bound.

Second, we have the spiritual authority to destroy the works of the devil!

1 John 3:8: He who sins is of the devil, for the devil has sinned from the beginning. For this purpose the Son of God was manifested, that He might destroy the works of the devil.

2 Timothy 2:26: And that they may come to their senses and escape the snare of the devil, having been taken captive by him to do his will.

My presupposition is that the ultimate purpose of the church is to destroy the works of the devil now, in this present age, unshackling souls locked in hell's power. The Spirit of the Lord is upon me to preach to the poor and the brokenhearted and proclaim liberty to the captives. I have the spiritual calling, power and authority to destroy the works of the devil. I have been called to break the bands of barrenness off my church by moving strategically into a pastor-evangelist anointing and function.

Do the Work of an Evangelist

As pastors or leaders of influence in our specific churches or places of ministry, we are responsible to "do the work" of an evangelist: to present the message of the gospel to the twenty-first century in terms and ways people will grasp and to provide people with an opportunity to respond:

> But you be watchful in all things, endure afflictions, do the work of an evangelist, fulfill your ministry (2 Tim. 4:5).

> Keep your eye on what you're doing; accept the hard times along with the good; keep the Message alive; do a thorough job as God's servant (*The Message*).

If the pastor doesn't move the church into a new realm of spiritual growth, who will?

Other researchers in the area of evangelism have come to the same conclusions. George Barna, in his book *Evangelism That Works* says, "First our research discovered that in almost every case the driving force behind evangelism that works and evangelistic ministry was the intense desire of the senior pastor to emphasize evangelism."[1]

Dr. Armstrong agrees: "One painful conclusion I reached long ago and have not had reason to modify after many years of trying to help churches accept and fulfill their ministry of evangelism is that the bottleneck in the process is often—if not usually—the pastor. It may be theoretically possible, but it is highly improbable, that any congregation will accept its corporate evangelistic responsibility without the active leadership, support and involvement of the pastor."[2]

The Pastor's Challenge to Attain Conversion Growth

My first step in breaking the bands of barrenness is to accept my role in leading the church into a new realm of fruitfulness. There are a number of challenges that leadership will face in moving a church from transplant Christian growth to unchurched, unsaved conversion growth.

The Challenge of Changing Our Mind-set
The pastor who is consumed with research, teaching, preaching, counseling and administration may need to balance these functions with a new level of pastor-evangelist ministry. Some pastors have a genuine, sincere conviction, rationally conceived, that evangelism is not everyone's responsibility, gifting or calling. This philosophy purports that if a person does not feel called to evangelism or equipped to do it, then that individual has no obligation to be a pastor-evangelist.

Second Timothy 4:5 clearly states that we are to do the "work" of an evangelist, that is to discharge all the duties of this ministry. Pastor-evangelists are to fully perform all the aspects of gospel work, beginning with a new conviction that "I am responsible" and a new desire of "Let's make this happen!" A pastor may have the desire but not the ability to move the church in a new direction. When this is the case, find a model to follow, seek counsel, read, pray, ask other pastors who are moving in this direction. Just don't give up before you get started!

The Challenge of Evaluating Our Programs
Pastors who are convinced that they can invade hell to give up souls and that their churches are meant to grow by conversion growth will strategically change the internal programs of their churches to match this conviction. If you are among those who want to see a new bent toward conversion growth, limit the number of competing internal ministries and programs that are supported by the church, thereby emphasizing the significance and centrality of evangelism. This may be difficult at first, as many church people are committed to church programs that bear little or no Kingdom fruit. It may mean reevaluating the enormous amount of time invested in choirs, social events, musicals and fellowship programs.

The Challenge of Breaking the Management Mentality
The pastor-leader who is consumed with a "management of excellence" syndrome will be detailed to death. A sure way to

guarantee a maintenance mentality is to allow management ideas to become the controlling factor in moving the church in any direction. Details should be considered, but they should not control. Excellence is honorable in balanced measure, but excellence is not the end. It is a means. Excellence is not the goal—

☯

Excellence is honorable in balanced measure, but excellence is not the end....Excellence is not the goal—souls are!

☯

souls are! Christ died for people, not excellent logos, papers, bulletins, carpet, chairs, buildings, lands and machinery. We as pastors are called to preach the gospel, not administrate the gospel. Management is needed. Administration is a necessity, but let's put it into perspective. What is the purpose of the church? This purpose should set some standards and prioritize our goals. What is it we are to give ourselves to more than anything else? What is my biblical purpose? These questions answered properly will motivate my schedule and my sacrifices.

The Challenge of Maintaining Balance

The pastor seeking to move into a pastor-evangelist ministry will need to keep the balance of a nurturing church and an evangelistic church. This is a challenge that defeats the attitudes of some before they even try. It's impossible! It's impossible, or at least very difficult to have two motors running at the same time—an evangelistic motor and a nurturing motor. If you move too far evangelistically, the church will be doctrinally shallow. If you move too far into the nurturing model, the church will be strong but sterile.

Balance is possible! Wise leadership is the key. Pastors who know how to equip leaders to do both jobs and keep both motors running will succeed. The pastor-evangelist is called to "equip" the saints to do the work of the ministry, to be an enabler of others, a wise implementer. Making disciples is part of the mainstream of church life, not a department of the church or the responsibility of a few highly motivated individuals. Equipping the saints is what the church does! When discipling is isolated from the mainstream of church thinking and life, evangelism may go without nurturing, which allows for a weak and shallow church.

The Challenge of Making Disciples

The pastor-evangelist sees clearly the vision of making disciples, not just reeling in decisions. A decision to receive Christ calls for a brief verbal commitment, a response without full knowledge of the cost, an emotional response more than a spiritual one. Making a disciple calls for a commitment, an incorporating of the new believer into the church life and ministry. The call to discipleship is a call to deepened character, a putting away of the old life, a lifestyle change that moves a person toward Christian maturity. The pastor-evangelist understands the biblical concept of lostness. Heaven, hell and the eternal state of the unbeliever motivates the leadership toward the gospel as a message that must be preached (see Matt. 28:19; Mark 16:15; Luke 24:47,48).

The Challenge of Moving from a Sunday Church to a Seven-Days-a-Week Church

Moving from a traditional "Sunday morning preaching" church to a "seven-days-a-week with all believers fulfilling their calling and responsibility as sharers of the gospel church" is a long stretch for many. The changes in the church must begin with changes in the pastor and influential leaders. Barrenness can be broken but it will not automatically drop off, disappear or evaporate.

Barrenness has causes and remedies. One cause of barrenness is a pastor without vision or heart to see the unsaved find Christ and to be assimilated into a spiritually alive and growing church. The pastor's heart is a key, and changing the heart begins with changing perspective. In his book *Today's Pastor*, Barna says, "I don't think any pastor truly committed to the gospel could look at America today and claim we're really revolutionizing this country."[3]

The pastor's eyes must be opened with new light that causes a new motivation, a new energy, a new reason for being in the ministry. Ministry is more than keeping the programs running, the budget balanced, the people happy and the offerings coming in. We all know that, but we can get trapped in our ministry routines. Bill Hybels asks a poignant question, "If there really is a heaven and a hell, then why doesn't anyone do anything for that neighborhood we can see right from the church window?"[4]

Changing Attitudes Toward the Lost

Bill Hybels's question calls for a leadership response, one that will move from the leader's heart into the heart of the church. When a leader begins to pray daily for the lost, something spiritual transpires. A new compassion arises; a new understanding and interest in lost people emerges. Interest grows in how they think, what they like and don't like. New sensitivity is cultivated toward the lostness around us.

This new heart attitude will then be reflected in the pastor's spiritual menu. What the pastor feeds the sheep will reveal a new burden to reach the lost. Shifts will occur—not only in spiritual diet, but also in staffing strategy, church programs, the church atmosphere and the church budget. Hybels says, "Despite large numbers of lost people in their vicinity, churches were all geared up to save the already convinced. Everything that happened—the teaching, the budgets, the services, the programs—were all designed for those who were safely inside the family of God. As a result, nobody from the neighborhood across the street ever went into the church."[5]

Shifting the Church Function and Budget

We have set aside money for buildings, staff secretaries, counselors, custodians, groundskeepers and youth pastors. What about money for reaching our Jerusalem? We have a responsibility to break the bands off of our finances and channel them toward the purposes of God. The shift in our spending will help the church to realize the shift in our priorities. We must adjust our budgets to match our evangelism vision.

We must make a shift in priorities from a maintenance mentality to a growth mentality. We must press hell to give up souls and move from adding people to the church to the principle of multiplication (see Acts 2:47; 6:1,7; 9:31). The church is the vehicle for reaching the world: people reaching people, people discipling people into thriving local churches. We must restore the biblical concept of "people lostness" and not allow lukewarmness to infiltrate our attitudes about hell and heaven. The eternal state of every living human being is at stake. An erosion of the truths of eternal separation and the horribleness of hell has occurred. The way to reverse its effects is to move from pastor-teacher to pastor-evangelist.

Understanding the Meaning of Evangelism

As we move from pastor-teacher to pastor-evangelist, evangelism must take on a new depth, a new meaning, a new reality. So what do we mean when we say, "evangelism"? The following quotes help to shed some light on the subject:

> Evangelism strictly speaking is the proclamation or presentation of the gospel of Jesus Christ to persons in this secular age so that they will understand its crucial and relevant significance and respond to Him as Lord and Savior in faith and obedience, identify themselves with the Christian community and serve Him in daily life and relationship.[6]

> The ministry by which a congregation shares The Faith, makes new disciples, and thereby becomes contagious is called "evangelism," or sometimes "evangelization." Whatever else one might mean by evangelism, one must necessarily mean the "making of new disciples."[7]

Evangelism is the bridge we build between our love for God and our love for other people. Through the work of the Holy Spirit, through us, God can complete His transformation of a person for His purposes and glory.[8]

Storming the Gates of Hell Through Prayer

The church with vision for the lost has begun to break the bands of barrenness (see Isa. 43:5,6; Matt. 16:16-18), but breaking barrenness does not stop with vision. The church must move forward into intercessory prayer and actually pray for the lost. Those who willfully resist the grace of God in order to do their own will and serve Satan will be eternally punished in hell, Satan's dwelling place. Hell is the place or state of final judgment of the wicked and of all who die in their sins and unregenerate state.

Hell is a terrible place of separation from the presence of God, from Jesus, from the holy angels and from the redeemed. No light, no life, no peace, no joy, no righteousness and no salvation will be there—only darkness and torment of conscience for those who have rejected and despised the grace of God. This dark abyss is the hell Jesus Christ died to save us from, and why the Living Church intercedes for the lost with passion and faith, storming the gates of hell.

Let us press hell together to give up souls:

Give up the spiritually blind (see John 12:40);
Give up the prodigals (see Luke 15:11-24);
Give up the futile and fools (see Rom. 1:21,22);
Give up the deceived (see Rom. 1:23-25);
Give up those given over to degrading, unnatural
    passions (see Rom. 1:26,27);
Give up those with a depraved mind (see Rom. 1:28-32);
Give up those under sin (see Rom. 3:10-18);
Give up the demon-possessed (see Matt. 17:18);
Give up those trapped by Satan (Rom. 16:20).

Cry out in prayer, "Give them up! Do not keep them back! Release them; let them go!"

Lessons from the School of Barrenness

In this chapter we have discovered that:

- One form of barrenness churches may experience is seeing only transplant growth or biological growth, not growth through sinners being saved.
- Pastor-evangelists must be about releasing our churches into creative, powerful new forms of "city reaching" and "city reaping."
- When we really believe it is our duty to reach the unsaved, our churches will reflect that conviction in the way we spend our time, allocate our money and structure our services.
- The pastor-evangelist sees clearly the vision of making disciples, not just reeling in decisions.
- When a leader begins to pray daily for the lost, something spiritual transpires. A new compassion arises; a new understanding and interest in lost people emerges. The pastor's heart becomes the heart of the church.
- The shift in our spending will help the church to realize the shift in our priorities. We must adjust our budgets to match our evangelism vision.
- Evangelism is the bridge we build between our love for God and our love for other people.
- The Church should be storming the gates of hell through prayer, but few people are committed to praying for the lost.

(((Making It Personal)))

1. How much of the growth in your church has come from true conversion growth? What changes are you willing

to make to ensure that you are not just sheep swapping?

2. Are you getting decisions for Christ or making disciples? What are some of the ways you can deepen the maturity level of those who have made decisions for Christ?

3. What does your church budget say about your commitment to world evangelism?

4. How much time are you personally investing in intercessory prayer for the lost? How is this amount of time reflected in your congregation's commitment to prayer for the lost?

Notes

1. George Barna, *Evangelism That Works* (Ventura, Calif.: Regal, 1995), p. 89.
2. Richard Stol Armstrong, *The Pastor as Evangelist* (Philadelphia, Pa.: Westminster Press, 1984), p. 13.
3. George Barna, *Today's Pastor* (Ventura, Calif.: Regal Books, 1993), p. 87.
4. Bill Hybels, *Rediscovering Church* (Grand Rapids: Zondervan, 1995), p. 16.
5. Ibid., p. 52.
6. Elmer G. Homrighausen, *Rethinking the Great Commission in an Age of Revolution* (Richmond, Va.: St. Giles Presbyterian Church, 1968).
7. George G. Hunter III, *The Contagious Congregation* (Nashville, Abingdon, 1979).
8. George Barna, *Evangelism That Works* (Ventura, Calif.: Regal, 1995), p. 27.

16

Changing Church Atmosphere

○

Keep watch over yourselves and all the flock of
which the Holy Spirit has made you overseers. Be
shepherds of the church of God, which he bought
with his own blood.

—*Acts 20:28*

Traveling allows me to experience many different kinds of cultures, cities, nations and places. Each has its own atmosphere. At times it might be unexplainable, like the atmosphere in certain cities where you can feel the impurity, perversion and the forces of hell in the air. My first time in Bangkok, Thailand, I encountered such a presence of evil, a pressure that settles down upon you although nothing is actually seen with the natural eye. It's an unseen atmosphere.

In my visits to countries that have temples where idol worship is active, the atmosphere is heavy with the stale smell of food and incense and the sound of bells and chanting. A heavy, dark, oppressive hopelessness hangs in the air. The atmosphere does not inspire me to pray, worship or smile. Atmosphere has the power to move my emotions, penetrate my thought processes and shape me during that moment. Atmosphere is actually a very powerful force in our lives, our families, our society and our churches.

Understanding the Power of Atmosphere

The word "atmosphere" means a pervading or surrounding influence or spirit, general mood or social environment. Atmosphere is affected by décor, music, art and spirits (see Eph. 6:10-12). Atmosphere may be affected by a carnal, confused mind, by demonic forces of evil or by the Holy Spirit of God.

The atmosphere of a barren church will be distinctly different from that of a church that is alive, growing and filled with signs of life. A barren church atmosphere might be stale, stagnant, boring, confusing, judgmental, legalistic and out of touch with people. A barren church atmosphere can be detected in every aspect of the church's expressions: the worship, preaching, offering, prayer, pastoral departments, the youth, children and so on. All these expressions will carry the same basic tenor as the overall church atmosphere.

A church that has broken the bands of barrenness and is experiencing the life flow of God will see a change in its atmosphere. The pastor-leader should take special interest in keeping the atmosphere conducive to a life flow of God. Scripture offers leaders several examples of a life-producing atmosphere:

- God in the Garden: An Atmosphere of Communion (see Gen. 3:8; 18:17-33; Exod. 25:22; Num. 7:8,9);
- God on the Mountain: An Atmosphere of Faith (see Gen. 22:13-19; 2 Chron. 3:1; Rom. 4:20,21; Heb. 11:17-19; Jas. 2:21-23);
- God in the Prison: An Atmosphere of Hope and Vision (see Gen. 37-41);
- God in the Secret Place: An Atmosphere of Awesomeness (see Gen. 28:10-22; Exod. 2:14; 3:6);

- God in the House: An Atmosphere of Worship
  (see 1 Chron. 5:13,14);
- God in the Prayer Meeting: An Atmosphere of the
  Supernatural (see Acts 2:1-4; 4:1-10);
- God in the Corporate Gathering: An Atmosphere of
  Spiritual Awareness
  (see 1 Cor. 12; 14).

Leaders Affect the Atmosphere

So who is responsible for the atmosphere of a church? The pastor and, of course, other influential leaders within the congregation. The pastor's perspective concerning God's presence, God's promises, spiritual warfare, life, ministry and the Holy Spirit will contribute to establishing the spiritual atmosphere of the congregation.

I am not elevating the pastoral gift above the others listed in Ephesians 4:11,12: apostle, prophet, evangelist and teacher. When I speak of the pastoral office, I realize the office could be occupied by one of the other gifted leaders as stated in Ephesians 4:12. The spiritual oversight of the local church is what I am referring to when I use the word "pastor." This person, this spiritual office, does carry a shaping influence over the congregation and upon the spiritual atmosphere in the church. Therefore, the pastor should approach every service with an:

Attitude of Faith: *I expect God to do something great today.*
Attitude of Love: *I have an overflow of godly love to give out
    today.*
Attitude of Satisfaction: *I bring to this service a sense of peace.*
Attitude of Enjoyment: *I love what I do, I love God and I enjoy
    the ministry and the church.*
Attitude of Team: *I desire all gifts and ministries to function.
    I encourage participation, not control.*

These attitudes are only a few that a leader is encouraged to develop and deposit into the church every time the church gathers. These attitudes will help to shape the other leaders and those people involved with the public church service.

Atmosphere Affected
by Legalism

Atmosphere change is absolutely necessary in moving a church toward harvesting lost people. It requires the change of spiritual attitude, perspective and passions in the church as a whole in all essential areas. This climate change may need to take place in some traditions of the church. Legalism, a rule-based rather than

Grace heals the wounds, but does not condemn people for being wounded. Grace blesses without requirements; legalism has so many requirements that people cannot get blessed.

a relationship-based way of relating to God, creates a climate uninviting to spiritually dead people. External legalism that requires certain dress, actions or attitudes of lost people needs to be visited by the love and grace of God.

Legalism—A Detectable Attitude

Legalism is an attitude, although it involves control, motive and power. Legalism in the church can be rooted in church pride. It can be an obsessive conformity to an artificial standard for the purpose of exalting self. Legalism assumes the place of authority and pushes it to unwarranted extremes, resulting in an illegitimate form of control that requires unanimity, not unity. This church stronghold must be removed if the spiritual climate is going to be changed.

The grace of God must become a prevailing, dominant atmosphere in the leader and other believers because a grace climate is inviting to the unsaved. Grace heals the wounds, but does not condemn people for being wounded. Grace blesses without requirements; legalism has so many requirements that people cannot get blessed. The motive for obeying the laws of Christ under grace is gratitude because we have been blessed, rather than in order to be blessed. In the New Covenant we work from a position of blessing to a position of obedience because of the blessing in which we have already been established.

Not Legalism, Not Cheap Grace

We need to be aware of legalism that robs Christians of their true freedom in Christ, and of the cheap, greasy grace that falsely offers freedom outside of scriptural boundaries. The church climate must be permeated with a biblical dose of New Testament grace. Throughout the New Testament, the predominant thought is the grace of God in Christ which redeems us, governs us and gives us everlasting consolation and good hope.

Grace is the peculiar property of true Christianity, a much needed trait in the twenty-first century. Grace depends on true Christianity for the realization of its full meaning and elevation to its rightful place. Grace was the focus of Christ's mission and He Himself was the embodiment of grace (see John 1:14,16,17). Acts 4:33 reads: "And great grace was upon them all." This was the climate of the first-century Church—great grace (see Acts 11:23; 13:43; 14:3,26; 15:11,40; 18:27; 20:24; 26:32).

The most important stage in the development of the New Testament doctrine of grace is the writing of the Pauline Epistles. For Paul, grace was fundamental to all his thinking. All of Paul's epistles open and close with a mention of grace (see Rom. 1:5,7; 16:20,24). The grace of the New Testament is God's unmerited favor demonstrated in the gift of his Son who offers salvation to all, who gives to those who receive Him as their personal savior an added grace for this life and hope for the future.

Seven Essential Elements for an Evangelistic Atmosphere

In his book *The Antioch Effect*, Ken Hemphill gives the following seven essential elements for developing a climate of evangelism:

1. Conversation about evangelism is natural. It is heard from the pulpit, the educational teachings, and laypeople. It is embodied in the prayers of the church. The church is saturated.
2. The evangelistic church is marked by a pervasive spirit of love. The pastor and all church leadership and church members openly express their love for the Lord, for one another and for the lost. There exists a deep level of caring in the church.
3. A spirit of expectancy and excitement permeates the evangelistic church. The church members come to the services expecting the Spirit of God to give a regular harvest of souls. You can sense the excitement when you walk onto the grounds of the church.
4. A sense of urgency motivates the people to be serious about outreach. A sense of urgency comes from a clear understanding of human lostness and the absolute necessity of salvation.
5. The evangelistic church has strong conservative theology and the activity of the church is ultimately based on doctrine. A clear teaching of heaven, hell, the eternal state of every soul and the righteous character of God to righteously put a soul in hell who will not accept the work of the Cross are essentials to motivation.
6. The evangelistic church expects God to work supernaturally. Many churches are paralyzed by their inability to believe God can supernaturally change lives. Any life submitted to God is submitting to a chance for a miracle.
7. A team spirit and a shared vision mark the evangelistic church. The pastor is not viewed as the hired gun

responsible for all evangelistic activity. The laity understands that all believers are responsible for fulfilling the Great Commission.[1]

To break the barrier of the unsaved community, we must assess our own church climate or church-ministry atmosphere. Every place has a felt atmosphere. We may not always be able to put our finger on exactly what the atmosphere is, but it is there. Change that atmosphere into a place that both believers and nonbelievers respond to because of the love, grace, mercy and sincerity found there and you will have an evangelistic church. Churches that grow have an alive, spiritual atmosphere that makes people want to be in church. They are drawn to it.

A church that has broken the bands of barrenness has:

- An atmosphere of open heavens, no spiritual hindrances.
- An atmosphere of unified expectancy, no business as usual services.
- An atmosphere of expecting supernatural surprises, no common, ordinary God to serve.
- An atmosphere in which everyone can receive, no unbiblical limitations on anyone.
- An atmosphere where people are honored and valued, no person is unimportant.
- An atmosphere of victory where winning in life is possible and God is able to do anything.
- An atmosphere of offensive and aggressive Christianity, not one that is defensive and "holds the fort."
- An atmosphere of giving liberally without selfishness and small thinking, no excuses or apologies.

This life-producing, love-giving, grace-pumping atmosphere is what the church needs now to revive those who are barren and to produce the fruit of the endtimes harvest. Let's move beyond barrenness by diagnosing our blockages, remedying our unhealthy attitudes and adjusting our impure motives so the birthing chambers of God's celebration houses are bursting with new babes in Christ and healthy families to care for them.

Lessons from the School of Barrenness

In this chapter we have discovered that:

- The atmosphere of the church is the responsibility of the pastor-leader.
- Atmosphere is affected by décor, music, art and spirits.
- Barren churches are often marked by legalism, an illegitimate form of control that requires unanimity, not unity.
- A barren church atmosphere can be detected in every aspect of the church's expressions: the worship, preaching, offering, prayer, pastoral departments, the youth, children and so on.
- A life-giving atmosphere is a grace climate. Grace heals the wounds, but does not condemn people for being wounded. Grace blesses without requirements; legalism has so many requirements that people cannot get blessed.
- The motive for obeying the laws of Christ under grace is gratitude because we have been blessed, rather than in order to be blessed.
- Churches that grow have an alive, spiritual atmosphere that makes people want to be there. Both believers and nonbelievers respond to the love, grace, mercy and sincerity found there.

((Making It Personal))

1. What is the atmosphere of your church? In what ways do you need to loosen up, love more and extend more grace and mercy to your staff and congregation?
2. Are there any areas in your church where legalism has crept in? Where are you too controlling?

3. Are you motivated by the blessings you have received, or by the blessings you hope to gain?
4. Does the atmosphere of your church reflect an attitude of gratitude for what Christ has done? What prevents you from fully surrendering your worship and praise to God?

Note

1. Ken Hemphill, *The Antioch Effect* (Nashville: Broadman Holmes Publishing, 1994), pp. 164-165.

OTHER GREAT BOOKS BY FRANK DAMAZIO

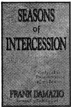

Seasons of Intercession

Seasons of Intercession emphasizes the role of intercessory prayer for every believer's life. Damazio demonstrates prayer strategies that will turn ordinary prayers into effectual intercessors. He shows how to be an intercessor individually and how to become a powerful intercessory church corporately.

ISBN: 1-886849-08-0

Effective Keys to Successful Leadership

Effective Keys to Successful Leadership describes the "set-man" model for building an effective leadership team and a healthy local church in the twenty-first century. Damazio builds his case for what it takes to be a successful leader in a luke-warm, confused, compromising, and religious atmosphere.

ISBN: 0-914936-54-9

Seasons of Revival

Seasons of Revival offers fresh insight and biblical thought to understanding seasons of God's outpouring. This book outlines the current need for revival, and develops the desire to see revival take place personally and then corporately and gives keys to sustaining revival long term.

ISBN: 1-886849-04-8

The Vanguard Leader

The Vanguard Leader sets a new standard and charts a clear course for those navigating the troubled waters leading into the twenty-first century. Damazio defines the characteristics, functions and motivation of vanguard leadership and encourages leaders everywhere to break free from past stagnation, mediocrity and complacency.

ISBN: 0-914936-53-0

LEADER TO LEADER TRAINING

The Making of a Leader

The Making of a Leader lays out a broad & deep discussion of what it means to be responsible for a group of "followers." This perennial bestseller presents a scriptural analysis of the philosophy, history, qualifications, preparation and practice of Christian leadership.

ISBN: 0-914936-84-0

Timothy Training Program

Taken from I & II Timothy, the *Timothy Training Program* pro-vides teaching materials for pastors and leadership trainers to use in equipping potential leaders. This package incorporates teaching, discussion, and relational hands-on discipling.

Teacher's Manual
ISBN: 0-914936-12-3
Student's Manual
ISBN: 0-914936-13-1

Lay Pastor Training Program

Designed to help train lay pastors to help alleviate the heavy ministry load of elders and the senior pastor, this course teaches lay people to do the harvesting and pastoring at a relational level within the local church.

Teacher's Manual
ISBN: 1-886849-05-6
Student's Manual
ISBN: 1-886849-06-4

Available at your local Christian Bookstore

For a complete catalog of resources call
BT Publishing 1-800-777-6057